Advance Praise for *Angel Cats*

"How wonderful that cats are finally being recognized as the excellent care-givers, companions, and guardians of the human species. And how perfectly presented is this recognition, through the skill and compassion of Allen and Linda Anderson. Once again, in their dedication to the animals who bless our lives, they have crafted a beautiful volume to be kept close at hand for inspiration and to be shared with everyone."

— Rita M. Reynolds, author of *Blessing the Bridge: What Animals Teach Us about Death, Dying, and Beyond*

"The engaging true stories in *Angel Cats* support a shift in perspective taking place around the world. More and more people are discovering that animals are not inferior, as argued by modern science, but are instead highly intelligent, spiritually evolved, and genuinely altruistic beings."

— Marta Williams, biologist, animal communicator, and author of *Learning Their Language*

"Angels come to us in many ways. Some are never identified, and some come to us and we don't even know they have changed our lives, maybe even saved us, until there is a realization. This enlightening book will make you take many a close look at your 'angel.'"

— Tippi Hedren, actress and animal activist

Praise for *God's Messengers*

"As a lifelong animal lover, I am delighted to see them celebrated in such a positive way. You and your pet will enjoy reading this together."

— Betty White, author and actress

"To speak of 'lower' animals is both arrogant and blasphemous. All traditional peoples have viewed animals as messengers and mediators of the divine, which is a lesson we need to relearn. *God's Messengers* is a bold reminder that consciousness takes many forms and is not restricted to humans."

— Larry Dossey, MD, author of
Healing Beyond the Body and *Healing Words*

"Animals truly are angels upon the earth, as Allen and Linda Anderson so beautifully remind us in their wonderful book *God's Messengers*. Their heart-opening stories are inspirational and remind us to take wonderful care of our animal friends."

— Doreen Virtue, PhD, author of
Messages from Your Angels and *Angel Therapy*

"Allen and Linda Anderson gracefully explore how we connect with the soul of the divine through soulful connection with our animal companions — beings who in this book emerge as messengers of immense beauty, humor, compassion, courage, inspiration, and love....*God's Messengers* reminds us that the keys to the kingdom can be found in our own homes, backyards, and barns."

— Linda Kohanov, author of
Riding between the Worlds and *The Tao of Equus*

"This sensitive book shows what is so obvious but what so few people see: that animals can be spiritual messengers and comforters and such a grace for us — and that God uses animals to help us all along our way. Thank goodness Allen and Linda Anderson are documenting this beautiful part of life for all to witness."

— Kristin von Kreisler, author of
For Bea: The Story of the Beagle Who Changed My Life

"Save yourself some time during this busy shopping season and pick up several copies [of this book] as gifts for all the animal lovers on your list. Yes, it really is that good!"

— *Best Friends* magazine

ANGEL
cats

Also by Allen and Linda Anderson:

Angel Animals: Exploring Our Spiritual Connection with Animals

God's Messengers: What Animals Teach Us about the Divine

ANGEL
cats

Divine
Messengers
of Comfort

Allen & Linda Anderson

NEW WORLD LIBRARY
NOVATO, CALIFORNIA

New World Library
14 Pamaron Way
Novato, California 94949

Front cover design by Cathey Flickinger
Text design and typography by Tona Pearce Myers

Library of Congress Cataloging-in-Publication Data
Anderson, Allen
  Angel cats : divine messengers of comfort / by Allen and Linda Anderson.
      p.   cm.
  Includes bibliographical references.
  ISBN 1-57731-448-4 (pbk. : alk. paper)
  1. Cats—Religious aspects. I. Anderson, Linda C. II. Title.
  BL443.C3A54 2004
  636.8—dc22   2004009696

First printing, September 2004
ISBN 1-57731-448-4

Printed in the U.S.A.

g A proud member of the Green Press Initiative

Distributed to the trade by Publishers Group West

10 9 8 7 6 5 4 3 2 1

Contents

Chapter Three
Were We Meant to Play with Our Littermates?

Chapter Four
Are Cats Mirrors of the Soul?

Chapter Five
Will We Hear the Sound of a Heavenly Purr?

Introduction

Stately, kindly, lordly friend,
Condescend
Here to sit by me, and turn
Glorious eyes, love's lustrous mead,
On the golden page I read.

— "To a Cat," Algernon Charles Swinburne

*W*ith velvet paws tucked serenely under his rhythmically purring body, an Angel Cat breathes sighs of contentment. Stretched out on the cushioned window seat in languorous repose, he gazes outdoors to watch birds and squirrels scurrying around in an attempt to entertain him. Then he turns away from the window and patiently scans his territory, where he spies an empty lap. Majestic as a prince, he rises and glides away from the window. Sauntering across the room, he prepares to take possession of the inviting thighs. He sits on the floor nearby with ears perked up expectantly and gazes intently at the lap, flicking his tail from side to side. Then he turns his head away as if indifferent to its allure. Suddenly, with the grace of a gazelle, he springs forward from his hind feet and leaps onto his rightful throne.

Confidently, his paws knead the lap as if it were made of yeasty dough that will rise into a soft pillow underneath him. The Angel Cat arches his back, twitches his whiskers, and gazes with lustrous eyes into the human's face. Within seconds, he closes his eyelids and luxuriates in the touch of fingers that lovingly caress his silky fur and rub his fuzzy cheeks. When the fingers stroke his face, his raspy pink tongue licks them gently, as if to congratulate them on having found their purpose in life. The soothing purr of this charming companion makes the human's cares and concerns float away on waves of vibrating sound.

When the petting is over, the Angel Cat rests. His front legs curl possessively around the human's knee, and his claws retract into the spongy pads of his paws. Immersing himself in the moment, he settles into a Zen-like meditative state.

For a tranquil minute, or maybe an hour, the cat awaits a tolling bell that only he can hear. It emanates from the mysterious cat consciousness and will announce when these peaceful moments must come to an end. Without a shred of regret, he silently leaps back onto the floor. Then he turns his head, nods, and solemnly winks at the person with whom he has shared this intimate respite. With soulful eyes and the detachment of a Buddha, the Angel Cat telegraphs the message that, as enjoyable as this moment in eternity has been, he has no need to cling to the exchange of pleasure. His friend's hands rest, lonely as winter tree branches, on the still-warm lap that no other earthly creature can fill as completely or sincerely.

Who are these mystical, mythical creatures that have captured our imaginations, blessing the earth with their elegant presence for three million years? How is it that, although they are a defined species, no two cats are alike? As Roger Caras says in *A Celebration of Cats,* "What cats are is individualistic. One of their most enchanting traits is that each one you meet really does require meeting."[1]

Why do cats fascinate us so thoroughly? Are they messengers who come into our lives as Divine instruments, to comfort us through the storms of life (the Greek word *angelos* means "messenger")? With their willingness to listen in silence and their frank, nonjudgmental gaze, do they assure us that no matter what is happening, everything truly is in Divine order? When they skitter around our homes with abandon or calculatingly stalk invisible prey, are they reminding us to approach life's challenges with creativity and flexibility? Is there something so extraordinarily spiritual about the cat kingdom that, if we observe, recognize, and apply what cats know, we can become more joyful, balanced, and loving human beings?

Cats have experienced the gamut from veneration to condemnation; they were worshiped as gods in ancient Egypt and executed as companions of witches in the seventeenth century. During the time of the Pharaohs, the entire human family mourned the death of its cat by shaving off their eyebrows to express deep loss, then mummifying and burying the cat's corpse in sacred ground.[2]

Throughout history, the beauty and grace of cats have inspired artists, writers, and musicians to immortalize them. Cats have been the subjects of poetry, nursery rhymes, novels (cat detectives), musicals *(Cats)*, and great works of art.

Then there is the spiritual nature of cats. According to Caras, "Legends said that at the moment of Christ's birth in the manger, a cat under the floor of the manger gave birth to kittens. That allegory has appeared again and again in paintings by Baroccio, Leonardo da Vinci, and other masters who depicted the Holy Family.... In the thirteenth century, cats were the only animals permitted to dwell with the sisters in English nunneries."[3] Buddhists consider cats to be symbols of self-possession. Though most of us have direct experiences only with *Felis cattus,* the small purring housecat, his cousin the lion continues to be respected for his godlike qualities. Elizabeth Marshall Thomas, writing about dwellers of the Kalahari in the 1950s, says, "The Bushmen recognized a supernatural quality in lions. The word for lion — *n!l* — like the name of God, could not be uttered in the daytime."[4]

In America today, housecats have taken possession of our homes and our lives. There are now 77 million cats in the United States, and Americans spend $31 billion a year on pet products.[5] We insist that hotels and airlines adopt pet-friendly policies so our cats can vacation with us. We buy French daybeds, multilevel towers, and scratching posts for our cats' sleeping, observing, and clawing pleasure. Without blinking an eye, we make appointments for them with chiropractors, acupuncturists, and masseuses. What is it about cats that ceaselessly fascinates us and makes them our essential companions?

We hope that *Angel Cats: Divine Messengers of Comfort* will convince you that, of all the feline qualities that have mystified humans throughout the ages, it is ultimately their spiritual nature that attracts us to these astonishing creatures. Their generosity, resourcefulness, compassion, and capacity for making the most of each moment shine through the pages of this book, revealing cats to be spiritual superstars. We're not going to inundate you with facts and figures or scientific studies. Rather, we will use the power of story to illuminate what cats teach us about the Divine, letting you draw your own conclusions.

In *The Story Factor: Secrets of Influence from the Art of Storytelling*, Annette Simmons retells an old Jewish teaching story that expresses our philosophy:

> Truth, naked and cold, had been turned away from every door in the village. Her nakedness frightened the people. When Parable found her, she was huddled in a corner, shivering and hungry. Taking pity on her, Parable gathered her up and took her home. There, she dressed Truth in story, warmed her, and sent her out again. Clothed in story, Truth knocked again at the villagers' doors and was readily welcomed into the people's houses. They invited her to eat at their table and warm herself by their fire.[6]

We invite you to warm yourself by the fire of Truth as you read this book, and to apply the lessons in each story to your own life. Allow yourself the catlike pleasure of savoring these true, often miraculous, accounts by reflecting on the meditations that follow them.

If you've ever lived with cats, you're sure to recognize their influence on

Speedy Anderson

our work. We wrote this book with the counsel and encouragement of our own cat companions. Speedy is a multicolored, big-hearted, train-engine-purring tabby. Cuddles is

his petite black-and-white adopted sister, who contorts her body into yoga-like poses while liberally and vocally dispensing wise opinions on just about everything. In the "Ask Cuddles" sections of this book, you'll be treated to some of this big-soul-in-a-tiny-body's thoughts, as interpreted by us.

So curl up with your own cat friends and anticipate a good read that may, at times, be startling and even a bit unsettling. Your cats will thank you for reading about their

Cuddles Anderson

brethren. They might dignify you with a lick and a purr if you begin to comprehend the extent of their spiritual nature. You'll become elevated (maybe even equal) in their eyes as you come to understand the purpose of cats. Your cat companions will be gratified as you realize why they have come into your life at exactly the right times and in just the right ways, bringing the special gifts that only cats can offer.

ANGEL
cats

CHAPTER ONE

Is Life Better When We Curl Up Together?

Two are better than one...
For if they fall, one will lift up his companion.

— Ecclesiastes 4:9–10

ats love us.

Did you know that meowing and purring express a unique relationship between humans and cats that has evolved over thousands of years? People don't read body language as skillfully as cats do, so living with us has taught our feline friends to get our attention and affection, which they seem to want and need, by vocalizing. Cats don't meow or purr much if a person isn't around to listen to them. Cats also adjust their vocalizations — higher, lower, softer, louder, more frequent, or more urgent — to tell us when they are hungry, frightened, hurting, or content.[1]

The extent of a cat's love for a human can be astonishing. In Jeffrey Moussaieff Masson's book *The Nine Emotional Lives of Cats,* he tells about a cat his sister encountered at a veterinarian's office. When she asked the vet why all four of the cat's paws were heavily bandaged, the vet explained that the cat's human had jumped from a ten-story window and died. The cat, in a desperate attempt to stop her friend from committing suicide, had hurled herself out the window right behind him. The cat had survived.[2]

Cats love us back.

We are the major source of food, shelter, and affection for housecats, and often for feral cats as well. When we belong to them, cats mark us and our homes with their scent, a brand as distinctive as the most expensive perfume. Some people feel that cats consider us to be their children, not the other way around.[3] Cats nurture, watch over, and play with us as if we were babes who didn't know how to take care of ourselves — and certainly didn't have a clue about when to indulge in a rollicking good time.

Cats love each other, too.

One night, Linda poured food into Speedy's bowl, then spaced out and forgot to move it from the countertop next to Cuddles's bowl and put it on the floor. Speedy is a big, elderly fellow, and he isn't able to climb up onto the counter. All evening, Cuddles, Speedy, and our dog Taylor fussed at Linda about something, but she couldn't figure out what they were trying to tell her. The next morning, when Linda went to feed everybody, she found that Cuddles had taken the situation into her own paws. She had somehow lifted Speedy's bowl of food and jumped off the counter with it. Without spilling its contents, she had placed the bowl on the floor, where it was supposed to be. Linda was grateful that Cuddles had taken such excellent care of her big brother, and resolved to be more present when feeding the cats.

The love of cats glows throughout this chapter. The first story, "One Lucky Cat," by Donna Francis, was the grand prizewinner in the Angel Cats contest, sponsored by Angel Animals Network, the organization we founded to use the power of story to increase love and respect for all life. Each of the succeeding stories demonstrates the true meaning of the words *love* and *friendship*. Cats' abilities to protect, to heal, to forgive, and to show loyalty have earned them a sacred place in humans' hearts and in the heart of God.

One Lucky Cat

Donna Francis
Whitewright, Texas

$\mathcal{A}$ week after Smokey, our family's barn cat, prematurely delivered a litter of kittens, my mother called to tell me that all but one of the kittens had died. Mom moved Smokey and her remaining kitten into the garage and promised to keep me posted. A couple of weeks later, Mom called again. She said that something was wrong with the remaining kitten, and Dad wanted to "put him out of his misery." Since I have a lot of experience volunteering for my local SPCA, Mom asked me to take a look at the kitten and tell her what I thought about his health.

When I arrived at my parents' home, I saw something unusual. Smokey was nursing a small, mouselike, three-week-old gray tabby kitten. The kitten had only one eye open, and his mouth was deformed. With a crooked stub of a tail and a drunken walk, he was much more uncoordinated than most kittens his age.

Although I was concerned about this kitten's tiny size and premature condition, I couldn't help noticing that he was a real character. Whenever he heard our human voices, he would leave his feline mom and seek us out. He followed us everywhere as fast as he could with his lurching walk. If anyone picked him up, he purred immediately. The tiny kitten seemed so happy that I convinced my parents to give him another week.

The next weekend, I drove back to my parents' home expecting to find that the kitten had deteriorated. He had indeed lost some weight, but he still showed the zest for life I'd seen in him the week before. I asked my parents to let me take the kitten home with me so that I could put him in with a group of orphaned kittens I was fostering for the SPCA. I made the offer with the stipulation that I would not keep the kitten; I already had two dogs and a cantankerous Persian cat who hated other male cats.

The week after I brought the kitten to my apartment, we visited the veterinarian. There, I was surprised to learn that not only was this kitten underweight, but the formula he'd been eating was causing him respiratory problems. The vet gave me suggestions on how to quickly graduate him to eating dry food. The vet also explained that this kitten had a cleft palate and nose and should have died at birth or shortly thereafter because kittens with this type of deformity usually can't nurse properly. The vet checked the kitten's closed eye and said that it would never open. The entire left side of this kitten's face had not developed, and his staggering walk suggested that he might have brain damage. The prognosis for the little guy was not good. The vet predicted that the kitten would not live past his first birthday.

I cried on the way home from the veterinarian's office. "What am I doing?" I wondered. "Does this kitten have any chance at all?"

When I came home, I put the kitten in the bathroom in a place I'd set up for the foster kittens. These babies were the kitten's age — four weeks old — yet he was only half their size and not nearly as well developed. With sadness in my heart, I wondered if the kindest thing would be to let my vet put this tiny, deformed creature to sleep. I went into the kitchen to cook dinner and think about what I should do.

As I made dinner, I noticed that Abbie, my toy poodle, wasn't underfoot as she usually is at dinnertime. I went to see what trouble she might be up to and was shocked by what I found. I had isolated the kittens from the rest of my four-legged family with a tall baby gate in the bathroom doorway. In the three years I'd been fostering kittens, the permanent residents of my household and the foster kittens had remained safely separated. However, I found Abbie staring intently at the baby gate. To my surprise, with one giant leap she landed on top of the gate and jumped over it to where the kittens were. I had no fear of her harming them, but I'd never seen her show any interest in

Donna's Lucky

the foster kitties. I silently watched as Abbie went straight to the deformed kitten and gently picked him up by the scruff of his neck. She climbed back over the baby gate with the kitten in her mouth and took him to my bed. There, she snuggled with the kitten and groomed him.

After a few minutes of tenderly caring for the kitten, Abbie looked up at me as if to say, "If you don't want to take care of him, I will. I won't give up on him." I guess you could say that, in that instant, Abbie made up my mind for me. The kitten was here to stay.

I never again isolated the kitten with the foster kittens; Abbie wouldn't allow it. If I tried to take the kitten to the bathroom, Abbie would grab him and carry him to my bed. (Not a good thing, since this little kitten wasn't litter-trained yet.) Abbie and the little kitten became inseparable; she took over his care and even protected him from my other cat.

In the meantime, my foster kittens were getting adopted and new foster kittens were arriving. No one who arrived as a prospective adopter seemed to be interested in a one-eyed, deformed kitten with breathing problems. Okay, so maybe I didn't try as hard as I could to find him a home, but I couldn't bring myself to upset Abbie by adopting out her baby.

Due to the respiratory problems caused by his cleft palate and nose, I had to take the kitten to the vet several times a month. At one point, he was even going to the vet twice a day for treatments. Each night, Abbie and I closed ourselves in the bathroom with the kitten and a vaporizer, just so this baby could breathe. Many nights I cried, fearing for the poor creature's life. I would listen to the kitten struggling for breath and wonder if it was cruel to keep him alive. But all I had to do was look into Abbie's eyes as she expressed her love for him, and I knew I was doing the right thing. "Don't give up on our baby," Abbie seemed to be saying. Our dedication was fueled by the mischievous sparkle that lingered in the kitten's eye.

Months after his arrival, I still had not named the kitten. Partly to spare my feelings, I was thinking, "I can't bear to name a kitten who might not survive." I had been through the pain of having foster kittens die, and I was not looking forward to feeling that kind of loss again.

With the vet's help and constant advice, we eventually got the kitten's breathing problems under control. I was delighted when he could go for an entire month without treatments. Finally, he was healthy enough to be neutered. On the day of the surgery, I realized that the perfect name for this kitten was Lucky. Yet I still had my doubts about what kind of life a sickly, deformed kitten would have. I needn't have worried.

As I write this story, Lucky is six and a half years old and weighs a healthy — even portly — sixteen pounds. Fortunately, he has no brain damage at all. When he sleeps by my head at night, though, it sounds like I'm with Darth Vader; Lucky's cleft palate makes him snore louder than most humans do. But I don't mind. Lucky still has that special swagger in his walk. My Persian cat didn't grow to love Lucky, but he also never tried to beat him up, as he had the other male cats I'd brought home. And, much to my amazement, this very special cat who had such a rough start in life has grown up to be an award-winning therapy cat.

I started taking Lucky to work with me at Jefferson Elementary School in Sherman, Texas, where I taught deaf children. There he began to share duties with Abbie, who is a registered therapy dog.

When Lucky came to school, he would greet everyone at the door with a loud "Meow!" If that didn't get my students' attention, Lucky would paw at their legs until they said hello or petted him. Then he'd sprawl out on the table and bask in the children's attention. My students loved it when Lucky decided that they'd worked long enough; he'd lie right down in the middle of their work. We called this "taking a Lucky break."

When Lucky purred, it excited my deaf students; they didn't have to hear it to know that they were making him happy. They could feel the vibration of his purring with their fingers, and they could see him shake. Lucky shakes when he is happy — which is most of the time, as long as someone is giving him attention.

Lucky also worked with the hearing students. One year, we had a writing contest in a first-grade classroom. The children were to write a short story about the therapy pet of their choice. Several students chose to write about Lucky. One low-achieving student, who hardly ever finished his work, turned in a story that won first prize. He was very proud of his story, but not as proud as I was. In his story, he'd written: "I love Lucky because he loves me, too."

Another of Lucky's volunteer jobs was at the Reba McEntire Center for Rehabilitation in Denison, Texas. He loved to lie on the clients' beds and feel their love. The clients and staff got a kick out of seeing a cat walking on a leash down the sterile halls of the center.

Lucky's deformities caused clients at the rehabilitation center to realize that their conditions could be worse. A client said, "Lucky reminds me of the saying 'I cried because I had no shoes; then I saw a man who had no feet.'" On one visit, a nurse came and got us out of a client's room; another client was upset because we'd skipped her room when she was asleep. By the time we arrived from the other end of the center, this client was out of bed and in her wheelchair, rolling down the hall to be sure she got to see Lucky. She took one long look at him and said, "My goodness, he's worse off than we are."

But perhaps one of Lucky's most important jobs was to teach people about differences — either their own or other people's. I helped Lucky write his own autobiography, which we still use to teach schoolchildren about accepting differences. I can only hope that the children learn the lesson Lucky lived to teach.

I didn't realize how effective Lucky and I were at conveying his message until the mother of one of my students related a story to me. This student was a beautiful little girl who was having trouble understanding why she was deaf and different from other kids. She would go home after Lucky's visits to our classroom and describe him and his antics to her father in detail. This was a wonderful way to expand her limited language skills, which was one of her educational goals. One day after she had described Lucky's visit, she said, "And he only has one eye. But that's okay, Daddy; he's different, just like me."

Lucky put in almost six years of hard, loving work before retiring due to the onset of carsickness. He isn't taking retirement well, as he now seems to feel neglected; I can't give him all the attention his clients used to give him.

Yet I think that Lucky has used up at least four of his nine lives. Looking back on Lucky's career, I'm amazed at how successful he was. In October 2000, Lucky was the co-winner of Delta Society's National Therapy Pet of the Year Award. Lucky and I flew to Boston to receive the award, and he was the only cat present. Highlights of Lucky's life story have appeared in newspapers, magazines (*Animal Wellness, Cat Fancy, Cats,* and *PetLife*), and a book (*The Healing Power of Pets,* by Dr. Marty Becker). He was featured in a segment of *Amazing Animals* on the Animal Planet network and on *Miracle Pets* on the PAX network. Lucky's photo even appears in the *2003 Cat-a-Day Calendar.* Lucky not only worked miracles; his entire life is a miracle. Lucky continues to inspire people to never let misfortunes or obstacles keep them from giving their best to life.

Meditation

Have you ever known a "different" or "special" cat? What has this cat taught you about valuing your own or others' uniqueness?

My Mother's Cat

Renie Burghardt
Doniphan, Missouri

$\mathcal{M}$y family lived in Hungary during World War II. When my nineteen-year-old mother died two weeks after giving birth to me, I inherited her cat, Paprika. He was a gentle giant with deep-orange stripes and yellow eyes that gazed at me tolerantly as I dragged him around wherever I went. Paprika was ten years old when I came into this world. He had been held and loved by my mother for all ten years of his life, while I had never known her, so I considered him my link to her. Each time I hugged Paprika tightly to my chest, I warmed to the knowledge that my mother had held him, too.

"Did you love her a lot?" I often asked Paprika as we snuggled on my bed.

"Meow!" he would answer, rubbing my chin with his pink nose.

"Do you miss her?"

"Meow!" Paprika's large yellow eyes gazed at me with a sad expression.

"I miss her, too, even though I didn't know her. But Grandma says Mother is in heaven and watching over us from there. Since you and I are both her orphans, I know it makes her happy that we have each other." I would always say these words to Paprika, for they were most comforting thoughts to me.

"Meow!" Paprika would respond, climbing on my chest and purring.

"And it makes me so very happy that we have each other," I would tell Paprika.

I'd hold him close, tears welling up in my eyes. Paprika would reach up with his orange paw and touch my face gently. I was convinced that this cat understood me, and I knew that I understood him. His love and devotion were always obvious.

My maternal grandparents raised me because the war had taken my young father away, too. He served in the army and visited me occasionally, but I could not live with him. As I grew older, the fighting intensified. Soon we were forced to become migrants in search of safer surroundings.

In the spring of 1944, when I was eight years old, Paprika and I snuggled in the back of a wooden wagon as we traveled around Hungary. During the numerous air raids of those terrible times, we had to scramble to find safety in a cellar, a closet, or a ditch. Paprika always stayed in my arms, for I refused to go anywhere without him. How could I ever be separated from him? After all, one of the first stories my grandparents ever told me was that my dying mother had begged them to take care of her cat as well as her baby.

After Christmas of 1944, when we were almost killed in a bombing, Grandfather decided that we would be safer in a rural area. We soon settled into a small house that had a cemetery as its neighbor. Grandfather and some helpful neighbors built a bunker for us nearby.

On an early spring day in 1945, we spent the entire night in that bunker. Paprika was with me, of course, because I refused to leave without my cat. Warplanes buzzed, tanks rumbled, and bombs whistled and exploded over our heads all night. I clung to Paprika, my grandmother held on to both of us, and we prayed the entire time. Paprika never panicked in that bunker. He just stayed in my arms, comforting me with his presence.

Finally everything grew deathly still, and Grandfather decided that it would be safe for us to return to the house. Cautiously, we crept into the light of early dawn and headed across the field. The brush crackled under our feet as we walked. I shivered, holding Paprika tightly. Suddenly there was a rustle in the bushes ahead. Two men jumped out and pointed machine guns at us.

"*Stoi!*" one of the men shouted. We knew the word meant "Stop!"

"Russians!" Grandfather whispered. "Stand very still and keep quiet."

But Paprika, who had never left me through all the traveling and the bombings, suddenly leapt out of my arms. So instead of obeying Grandfather, I darted between the soldiers and scooped up the cat. The tall, dark-haired young soldier approached me. I cringed, holding Paprika against my chest. To my astonishment, the soldier reached out and gently petted my cat.

"I have a little girl who is about your age," he said. "She's back in Russia. She has a cat just like this one." As he smiled at us, I looked up into a pair of kind brown eyes, and my fear vanished. My grandparents sighed with relief.

Later that morning, we found out that the Soviet occupation of our country was in progress. Many atrocities occurred in Hungary in the following months, but because the young soldier had taken a liking to me and my cat, our lives were spared. He visited us often and brought treats for Paprika and me. Then one day, a few months later, he had some news. "I've been transferred to another area, Malka ['little one'], so I won't be able to visit you anymore," he said. "But I have a gift for you." He reached into his pocket and pulled out a necklace. It was beautiful, and it had a turquoise Russian Orthodox cross on it. He placed it around my neck. "You wear this at all times, Malka. God will protect you from harm. And you take good care of your kitten."

I hugged the soldier tightly, then watched with tears in my eyes as he left.

Throughout the trying times that persisted in our country, Paprika's love made things easier for me to bear. He was my comfort and my best friend, and he rarely left my side.

In the fall of 1945, Grandfather went into hiding. He had spoken up about the atrocities taking place in our country, and he didn't want to be imprisoned as a dissident by the new Communist government. Grandmother and I expected Christmas to be solemn, but it then turned into my worst nightmare. I awoke on Christmas morning to find Paprika lifeless and cold, still curled up next to me. I picked up his body, held him close, and sobbed uncontrollably. He was nineteen years old, and I was only nine.

"I will always love you, Paprika. I will never give my heart to another cat," I vowed through my tears. "Never, ever!"

"Paprika's spirit is in heaven now with your mama, sweetheart," my grandmother said, trying to comfort me. But my heart was broken on that terrible Christmas Day.

Grandfather remained in hiding until the fall of 1947. At that time, we were finally able to escape Communist Hungary by hiding among some ethnic Germans who were being deported to Austria. When we got to Austria, we lived in a displaced-persons ccamp for four years. But there was hope for us: We were accepted for immigration to the United States of America. In September of 1951, we boarded an old Navy ship and were on our way to America.

Christmas of 1951 was our first in this wonderful new country. The horrors of war and the four years of hardship in a refugee camp were behind us. A new life, filled with hope, lay ahead.

On that Christmas morning, I awoke to a tantalizing aroma wafting through the house: Grandmother was cooking her first American turkey. Grandfather, meanwhile, pointed to one of the presents under the Christmas tree. The package seemed to be alive, for it was hopping around to the tune of "Jingle Bells" that was playing on the radio. I rushed over, pulled off the orange bow, and lifted the lid from the box.

"Meow," cried the present, jumping straight into my lap and purring. It was a tiny orange tabby kitten. When I looked into his yellow eyes, the vow I'd made in 1945 to never love another cat crumbled away, and love filled my heart again.

I do believe my mother smiled down approvingly at us from heaven that Christmas Day, while Paprika's spirit purred joyfully at her side. Since then, there have been many other cats in my life, but the memory of my mother's cat will live in my heart forever.

Meditation

Has a cat fulfilled a purpose in your life? Have you ever felt a Divine hand guiding a cat to give exactly what you needed?

Harley, the Cat Who Changed a Facility into a Home

Margie Broadrick, with photo by Kathryn Van Mater
Madison, Tennessee

I work at the Madison Healthcare and Rehabilitation Center, a long-term care and rehabilitation center in Nashville. It was there that I first met the abandoned kitten whom we staff members named Harley. Harley seemed to arrive at exactly the right time. Our previous resident cat had left a vacancy, and Harley — who became a specialist in offering love and comfort — seemed destined to take over the job.

I call Harley's work at the nursing home a "job" because a resident cat needs to have a loving, sensitive nature to do this kind of work. Our previous cat hadn't enjoyed caring for people; she disliked being touched, and would dart outdoors at every opportunity. But from the minute Harley arrived, he simply took over the previous cat's role and, in the process, transformed our facility into a home.

What are the requirements of Harley's job that he fulfills so well?

First, he willingly allows anyone to hold him at any time. I take Harley with me from room to room and let the residents pet him.

He enjoys the interaction. As their gnarled fingers stroke his beautiful smoky-gray fur, he looks up at them lovingly with his bright golden eyes. There is almost no limit to what Harley will tolerate if he thinks it will make someone feel better. But when Harley gets a bit tired of the attention, he looks at me with an expression that says, "I've had enough now." As I am the nursing home's activity director, it's up to me to give Harley a break then, and I do.

Second, Harley has forged a unique relationship with each resident and staff member. For example, he likes to ride on the shoulders of one of the LPNs (liscensed professional nurses) as he makes his rounds. He greets another nurse by jumping onto her car after she parks in the lot. He has the capacity to determine what each person needs and then, without reservation, to give it to them.

But perhaps the most important aspect of Harley's job is to spread his love around to people who need him most. Although he has no favorites, if someone doesn't feel well or is about to make a transition, Harley seems to sense that he is needed. He goes to the person's room and offers extra compassion and companionship. No matter how ill the patients are, they appreciate the fact that Harley is at their side, serving as a feline guardian angel.

Miss Anne was one of our spry residents until she suddenly became very ill. For two weeks, Harley curled up at the foot of her bed almost constantly. But when Miss Anne required privacy, such as when an assistant needed to change her undergarments, Harley would leave the room like a perfect gentleman. He would discreetly stroll into the hallway and wait patiently outside Miss Anne's door until he could return. As soon as the assistant left, Harley would resume his vigil. Even in the hours after Miss Anne had passed away,

Harley stayed in her room and brought great comfort to the deceased woman's two daughters.

Another time, Harley sensed that Mr. Clarence's condition had taken a downturn. The cat went to Mr. Clarence's room and sat on the chair next to the dying man's bed. There he stayed, waiting calmly, quietly, and angelically as Mr. Clarence crossed the threshold between life and death.

When Mr. John was terminally ill, Harley took on the mission of making the sick man laugh. The cat tumbled, chased his tail, and performed antics on the windowsill, always bringing a smile to Mr. John's face. The staff marveled at how much joy Harley brought to Mr. John. Even though Mr. John knew that his situation was very serious, Harley's visits lightened his load.

Margie's Harley

Our easygoing Harley understands how to relax and be in the moment. He is a great stress-reliever for the hardworking caretakers on our staff, and a role model who teaches us to take life in stride.

Every day, Harley reminds me that humans and animals are living beings who share this complex fabric of life. Feeling Harley brush gently against my leg during a stressful meeting or watching him leap boldly yet gracefully onto a table and stretch out languidly, inviting me to stroke his fur, helps relieve the tensions of my day. When I glance at Harley, in a deep, peaceful sleep on the floor of his kitty house with his feet dangling over the edge, I am reminded that life is to be taken seriously — but not too seriously. I hope that all of us who find peace and unconditional love through animals will be fortunate enough to have the comfort of a Harley in our final hours.

Meditation

Are there cats who have shown you how to listen, how to be present, and how to give what's needed without expecting anything in return?

The Persistent Princess

Christina Louise Dicker
Bunyip, Victoria, Australia

For three long years, I struggled to survive in an environment where I did not fit in. Although I loved my job at a large wholesale plant nursery, I felt isolated because I had little in common with the other employees. I have always been an optimist, blessed with abounding energy and enthusiasm for life and nurturing a deep love of nature. But many of my workmates were tired, downhearted, and bored with the monotony of their work: the constant repetition of potting hundreds of plants, day after day. Very few of them had time or compassion for their fellow humans, and less still for their fellow animal creatures.

When I first began working at this job, I befriended a small tortoiseshell cat who lived in the shed where I spent most of my working hours. Her coat was dark and shabby, but she had a pretty caramel-colored bib under her chin. She was a dainty thing with warm, olive-colored eyes and a soft feline voice that occasionally let out a little meow. This cat spent most of her time in the loft of the shed to escape the snapping jaws of the company owners' dog, a bull-terrier/blue-heeler cross. The dog had the run of the premises, and nobody seemed to care that she frequently terrorized the tortoiseshell cat. Before the cat was spayed, the family dog had mauled two litters of her kittens. To add to her suffering, the beleaguered cat barely survived an episode of snail-bait poisoning.

As a kitten, the tortoiseshell cat had been brought into this workplace for one reason: to catch mice. My employers had given her an ugly name and were never thoughtful about her care or feeding. I refused to call her by the ugly name, and instead renamed her Princess. A shy, petite creature, Princess was extremely affectionate. It surprised me that she managed to keep her sweet nature, because she was rarely treated with kindness.

My greatest pain was in observing the interaction between Princess and a woman named Jan. Jan was one of the oldest workers at the company, and she'd been there a long time. Her bitterness was obvious in each comment or facial expression, and she consistently held grudges against anyone who displeased her. I often watched as this dear cat attempted to rub up against — or, as we say in Australia, smooch against — Jan's legs, only to be kicked away. Many times I held my tongue — and a few times I didn't. On the few occasions when I spoke up against her insensitivity, my protests only angered Jan and put my feline friend in greater danger from her hostility. The issue of Jan's unkindness to Princess remained unresolved, and I stayed perpetually uncomfortable.

It frustrated me to watch Princess persevere with this coarse woman. I wondered why she persisted in approaching Jan when the painful outcome was always the same. I couldn't help but be concerned about Princess's emotional state: Was she terribly sad and lonely? Or was I merely projecting my own feelings onto her? I eased my anxiety with the thought that perhaps Princess didn't mind being mistreated as much as I thought she did.

Yet my empathy for Princess caused me to resent the people around me, and my negative feelings eventually blossomed into full-blown hostility. I was angry that nobody else seemed bothered by the continued abuse of the cat. I tried to offer some compensation by feeding Princess tidbits in an attempt to make her feel loved. I frequently told her how beautiful she was. She began to seek me out each day, and she seemed delighted to receive some badly needed affection.

As it turns out, the extra attention I gave Princess was therapeutic for both of us. The months passed. My attitude at work improved somewhat. I managed to avoid any further confrontations with employees.

Then one day, I witnessed something so wonderfully amazing that it filled me with joy and humility. I walked into work, and there was Princess sitting up on the workbench, eating a fancy brand of cat food. To my amazement, Jan had brought the food especially for Princess. Pleasantly surprised, I looked over at Jan. She smiled at me and said, "I took pity on her." I was completely taken aback by Jan's gesture of kindness toward my feline friend. "How could this be the same woman I've worked with for so long?" I wondered.

Christina's Princess

Witnessing this change of heart gave me great comfort and kindled a stronger acknowledgment of the spiritual qualities of animals. I then understood why Princess had never given up on Jan, even after so many harsh rejections. Princess possessed the strength of spirit to break through the shell of a hardened heart. At the same time, this cat gave me a reason and a way to resolve my bitterness toward a fellow human being. What a wise and powerful cat she must have been to make this miracle happen!

Several months after Jan had befriended Princess, my boss decided that he no longer wanted the cat. Knowing that I had formed a bond with her, he asked if I would like to take her away. My heart leapt at the opportunity to rescue this creature and give her a kind, loving home. The final outcome was a dream come true: I now have a patient, persistent Princess living with me as a special member of my family.

Meditation

What do cats teach us about how to break through the shell of a hardened heart? Has a cat inspired you to forgive someone who has wronged you?

The Most Remarkable Gift

Carole S. Cahill
City Island, New York

*S*andy was a large orange tabby with cotton-ball paws and eyes the color of peridot, a semiprecious stone that is lighter than emerald and clearer and brighter than jade. Sandy appeared at my back door one evening, wild, wary, and hungry. I offered him food, and he watched me until I moved away.

Sandy obviously had been someone's pet, because he seemed to be in pretty good shape. His eyes were clear, and he showed no scratches or nicks on his face or ears. He was clean, and his weight seemed healthy. Although he was wary and even frightened, he didn't show the terror of a wild animal, who would move out of range yet not out of sight. But Sandy ate like a stray, devouring his food with the cautious desperation of a creature who had neither a home nor the assurance of his next meal. As I watched him eat, I wondered what had happened to him. What cruelty or neglect had brought him to my doorstep?

After that first night, Sandy showed up every evening. He related to me under the implicit feline contract: He would grace me with his presence in return for food and my slavish devotion. Since Sandy was such a handsome, well-mannered gentleman, I naturally complied. I looked forward to his visits and enjoyed watching him. He apparently looked forward to his meals, too, because he always showed up ravenously hungry.

Sandy seemed to be growing more comfortable with me. He began to stand his ground rather than back away, and sometimes he started to eat before I closed the door. Eventually he must have begun to associate me with food, if not friendship, because he would look me straight in the eye and approach, waiting patiently for his dish. If he was in a particularly mellow mood, he would let me stroke his ear while he ate.

Over time, Sandy and I developed an amicable understanding of each other. With a grain of trust and an ocean of fear, he would arrive each night to devour my offerings. In return, he offered nothing more than his attendance. I felt flattered when he began to eat without waiting for me to withdraw. Sometimes he even stayed after his meal to wash himself or take a nap. His company delighted me, and he seemed reasonably comfortable. He sensed that he was in a safe place, but experience had taught this cat to maintain his independence.

Then one night, Sandy brought me the most remarkable gift. He again appeared at the back door, wild, wary, and hungry. But this time he seemed more cautious than usual, holding me in his gaze as if to say, "Don't approach." His glance flicked away for a moment. That's when I noticed that he'd arrived with a companion; a tiny kitten in a neat tuxedo scampered nearby.

I put out a dish of food. Sandy, lion-fierce, watched me as he guarded his charge, the gentle kitten. Sandy didn't eat, and his eyes hardly left me. His gaze warned me not to interfere with the kitten's mealtime.

Sandy was hungry, of course; he was always hungry. But he didn't eat. The kitten ate, and Sandy watched, neatly feline-folded and vigilant. Only after the kitten had finished her dinner and scrambled off to enjoy a safe space and a full belly did Sandy approach his own food.

Looking back at that incident, I imagine that Sandy knew I'd given him something, even if only some food and a place to stay whenever he wanted it. I know he gave me something far more precious: He showed me how beings can share with other beings. He'd found a hungry baby animal and chosen to share what little he had in this world with her. With extraordinary generosity and compassion, Sandy offered his food and safety to the kitten. And in the process, he taught me a lesson in fellowship.

Meditation

When someone needed something more than you did, has a cat demonstrated how to perform selfless acts? What has a cat taught you about sharing?

The Comfort of Cameo

Toni Eames
Fresno, California

Several years after my father died, my mother, whom we call "Mommala," decided that a cat would be the perfect companion. Mommala was still working and away from home for ten hours a day, and she didn't feel that a dog could be left alone that long. At the time, I shared my home in New York with two cats, Disney and Tevya, so Mommala considered me to be an expert on cats. We went to an animal shelter near Mommala's house in Queens, New York, where a lovely black-and-white one-year-old cat stole her heart. We brought the cat home and named her Cameo.

Mommala became extremely attached to her first feline friend, so when Cameo contracted feline leukemia virus a year later and died, Mommala simply had to get another cat. Our veterinarian, Dr. Tobias, was trying to place a litter of black-and-white six-week-old kittens at the time, and Mommala fell in love with a Cameo lookalike in miniature. She honored this new little bundle of fur by giving the kitten the name of her beloved predecessor.

The new Cameo spent the first eight years of her life as an only cat. However, whenever I traveled, Disney and Tevya stayed at Mommala's house. The three cats established a comfortable relationship during those times together, but Cameo was not as relaxed around dogs. Because I am blind, I often visited Mommala with my guide dog, Ivy; Cameo would spend the entire visit hiding under the bed. Mommala and I had a reciprocal catsitting arrangement, so whenever she traveled, Cameo stayed with me. During those visits, Cameo's inherent shyness caused her to hide behind the stove or on the closet shelf. Ivy was always gentle with cats, but Cameo remained uncomfortable around any member of the canine species.

When Mommala died in 1989, Cameo's world turned upside-down. My new husband, Ed, and I had moved to California, and we brought Cameo to live with us. Her old friend Disney was there, but Tevya had died and Kimmel, a white-and-black kitten, had been added to the family since Cameo had last stayed with me. Another major change Cameo had to face was the presence of Kirby, Ed's guide dog. It had been hard enough for Cameo to deal with my golden retriever, but now there were two of these playful creatures in the house.

Cameo's passion for food was the initial impetus for getting over her shyness. She loved to eat, and she quickly learned that there was no reward to be gained by hiding. Her strong desire to be cuddled and groomed also kept her in the midst of family activities. When she realized that large dogs could easily be dominated by a powerful hiss, she began to relax around our two guide dogs.

Over the next few years, Cameo coexisted with her canine and feline siblings. It didn't take her long to figure out that it was easy to leap over a dog to get to her favorite human lap. And when the alarm clock went off in the morning, Cameo made room for the canine corps to jump on the bed she shared with us.

Although Cameo and Ivy lived in harmony for six years, they

rarely interacted. By August of 1995, Ivy's health had significantly declined, and the quality of her life had deteriorated to the point where I knew our partnership had to end.

Toni and Cameo

One fateful day, I had to phone our vet, Dr. Larsen, and ask him to come over and euthanize my devoted partner and teammate of the past eleven years. As I hung up the telephone and began sobbing, fourteen-year-old Cameo sprang into action. She flung herself into my arms with a clear message that she felt my pain and was there to comfort me. When my tears dried, I sat on the floor, stroking Ivy. Cameo shared her ministrations with the dog, her long-term house partner. She walked back and forth between Ivy and me, purring loudly and stopping periodically to lick Ivy's face — something she'd never done before.

When Dr. Larsen and our friend Eve came to share Ivy's last moments, we all sat in a circle with Ivy in the center. Cameo, fast asleep by that time, awoke with a start and jumped over Eve to play her part. The cat lay facing Ivy with her paws touching the dog's. As we all watched, Cameo soothingly purred Ivy into death. Cameo's behavior on this tragic day was truly astounding. Not only did she comfort me, but she also tenderly ministered to my cherished guide as the life ebbed from Ivy's body.

Through sharing her compassion with me at a time of great

sadness, my little angel Cameo helped me cope with one of the most difficult transitions of my life. For that act of love and devotion, I am eternally grateful.

Meditation

With the love and compassion that cats often show for their fellow creatures, do they teach us how to minister to each other?

Ask Cuddles

Dear Cuddles,

Do cats really love us, or are we merely the source of their food supply?

> Sincerely,
> *A Human Can Opener*

Dear Can Opener,

Can't you tell we love you from the way we follow you around, jump onto your chest when you least expect it, and purr even when it's not dinnertime? Of course, we love you even more after you've given us our favorite cat food!

> Complexly yours,
> *Cuddles*

Are cats God's furry healers? In the next chapter, you will meet the health-care professionals of the cat kingdom. They offer prescriptions for wellness that are unmatched by any pharmaceutical product.

CHAPTER TWO

Do We Get Help to Heal Life's Scratches?

All your wondrous wealth of hair,
Dark and fair,
Silken-shaggy, soft and bright
As clouds and beams of night,
Pays my reverent hand's caress
Back with friendlier gentleness.

— "To a Cat," Algernon Charles Swinburne

As surely as human nurses and doctors tend to our wounds, cats heal us. Their presence can lower your blood pressure, lift your depression, and cause you to live longer. A cat's purr is perhaps one of the most amazing healing agents on earth.

In an article entitled "A Cat's Healing Purr," Dr. Lev G. Fedyniak, M.D., writes, "Having surgery? Perhaps after coming home, keeping a cat nearby will reduce your recovery time." To support this proposition, Dr. Fedyniak cites a study of forty-four cats by Elizabeth von Muggenthaler, a bioacoustics specialist at the Fauna Communications Research Institute in North Carolina. Von Muggenthaler found that the purring of an average housecat falls into the frequency range of 25 to 40 cycles per second (Hz). "Interestingly," Dr. Fedyniak observes, "research has shown that exposure to frequencies at...20 to 50 Hz induces increased bone density, relieves pain, and heals tendons and muscles....Many individuals swear they can ease or completely eliminate their migraine headaches simply by lying down with a purring cat next to their head."[1]

The stories in this chapter remind us that not only do a cat's healing powers often border on the miraculous, but they are given naturally and freely with no questions asked, no rewards required. Like the storytellers in this book, if you have received the gentle attention of a cat who loves you and longs to make you feel better, you have been kissed by the Divine.

God's Kitty Heart Specialists

Carol Smith
Saco, Maine

*O*ne foggy, rainy October day in 1992, I was walking along a beach road near my house and enjoying the crisp autumn air. Many of the summer vacation homes were closed for the season. With no other activity to draw my attention, I began to watch a black cat who seemed to be trying to keep her baby from running into the road. While she was herding her kitten, the mother cat was also chasing a bird. I chuckled at what this mother cat had in common with all human mothers I know. It is quite a task to protect your young while carrying out family responsibilities.

When I came closer to the cats, I realized by seeing their scruffy coats and thin bodies that they were in trouble. I asked neighbors about them. People told me these cats had been in the vicinity for a few days. All the while, the nursing mother cat had been desperately attempting to provide food for her baby.

I looked for more of this mother's kittens, but I didn't see any. Sensing that the creatures wouldn't survive much longer under these conditions, I scooped up the two orphans and brought them home with me. Little did I know that they would someday return the favor and contribute a crucial element to my health and well-being.

I named the cats Molly and Miss Minnie. After I fed Mother

Molly, who was only about six months old, she was able to better care for both her daughter and herself. This mother and daughter had a special relationship, yet they also had distinct personalities. From the moment when I first picked her up, Molly started to purr. Miss Minnie, tiny enough to fit into my shoe, didn't learn to purr for several months. The two cats seemed happy to be together. They played together often, and Molly washed Miss Minnie and herself for a good part of the day.

Carol's Miss Minnie and Molly

A few years after Molly and Miss Minnie had come to live with me, Molly started a strange new routine: Each night, she awakened me from a sound sleep. When I awoke, I'd notice that my heart was racing and my blood pressure and pulse were soaring.

I decided to see a doctor about my health, but even with prescribed medication I continued to feel poorly. On a few occasions, I passed out during the day; upon returning to consciousness, I found Molly licking my nose to awaken me. Molly continued to nurse me in this way as I went on with my busy life.

At one point, I noticed that Molly began to sleep closer to my head at night. I was sometimes awakened by her whiskers tickling my face as she brushed my cheeks and listened to my breathing. I'd roll over and go back to sleep, only to have Molly awaken me with her whiskers again. Around then, I began to take a new medication. When it began to help with my heart condition, Molly stopped waking me up at night, and I slept peacefully for many years.

Miss Minnie grew into a lovely, bushy-tailed, gray-and-black-striped coon cat with big paws. She looked much like her mother, although Molly was mostly black with a little white. Miss Minnie was not the kind of cat who would cuddle with me. In fact, after she was spayed she became aloof and self-centered.

I was surprised, then, when Miss Minnie started to change her standoffish ways. In the fall of 1997, when she was about five years old, Miss Minnie started to awaken me during the night. Just as the naturally loving and caring Molly had done years before, Miss Minnie began the strange ritual of walking up and down on top of my body to wake me up. At first I would check to see if she needed anything. It was perplexing to me that she never left my bed all night. If she woke me with her body walk and I didn't get up, Miss Minnie would sit on my chest and lick my face. It was as if Molly had taught her this routine.

There was an additional perplexing issue. Harold, an orange four-month-old male cat, had joined us in March of 1994. He was not healthy, physically or emotionally, and Miss Minnie resented it when Molly gave Harold her motherly attention. After all, Miss Minnie had been an only child. She didn't like the fact that Harold slept with me, and she usually jumped down when the intruder came onto the bed. But during the fall of 1997, Miss Minnie stayed by my side and continued to fulfill her mission, despite her resentment of Harold's presence on my bed.

My heart condition still seemed to be controlled by the newest medication, so I continued to work long hours at my job. Then one day, when I went for my usual beach walk, my heart began to race and beat irregularly. I managed to get back home and call a nurse friend. She checked on me and quickly whisked me to the emergency room.

After being admitted to the hospital, I was hooked up to a heart monitor. All that night, the nurses came in repeatedly to awaken me. I realized that this was what Molly and Miss Minnie had been doing for me over the years; my cat nurses must have known when my heart beat too rapidly or stopped beating during the night, and that was why they'd awakened me. Now that I was ill and had time to reflect, I realized that I had two cats who were angels. I thanked God that they had come into my life on that damp day in October years before.

In the summer of 2003, Miss Minnie started to sit on my chest again. It was uncomfortable. Even though I pushed her down, she always returned.

I changed doctors in September of 2003. After a visit to my new doctor, he called to say that the monitor I'd been wearing over the weekend showed that my heart was stopping for eight seconds at a time, several times each night. "You need surgery today," he said. I suddenly realized that this was what Molly and Miss Minnie had been trying to tell me by waking me up during the night and walking or sitting on my chest. After I explained to my cardiologist what these cats had done over the years, he said, "Your cats were pacemakers." I really believe that these wonderful animals served as my heart monitors. Until the doctor put an implant in my chest to monitor my heartbeat, my cats kept me alive.

Molly and Miss Minnie both remained my primary caregivers

Carol's Harold

throughout their lives. Over time, I've learned to listen to my kitty heart specialists more carefully. I discovered that they were far smarter about my health than I was. I also slowed down the hectic pace of my life. Molly and Miss Minnie seemed to know that I had started taking better care of myself, and they eventually showed less concern.

As it turned out, Molly also had a heart condition. She died in her sleep — a loss that is still painful to me. Sometimes it makes me sad to think that, had it been possible, an implant might have helped Molly, since she died with the same condition I had.

I am also thankful that Harold found his way into our lives. The doctors' treatments and Molly's love healed him, and now Miss Minnie and Harold have each other as companions. They both miss Molly very much. They consoled each other after her death, and for months Harold continued to call out for Molly.

As for my heart today, I know I'm doing better. Since my last surgery and the implant, Miss Minnie has not sat on my chest once.

Meditation

Molly and Miss Minnie became a healing team to keep their human charge alive for many years. What kind of teamwork and dedication is required for you to have a healthier life or to enable you to help someone else?

The Cat Who Made Amends

Carol L. Skolnick

New York, New York

*N*ot the most emotionally stable animal to begin with, my cat Amanda hated and feared children. Specifically, she was terrorized by anyone less than five feet tall or fourteen years old.

Wouldn't you know it? Children were always drawn to Amanda. Such a pretty kitty, she had huge yellow eyes and glossy, thick gray fur with a purplish tinge that begged to be stroked by little hands. But at the sight of a human child, Amanda would hiss, spit, get a fat tail, and dart to the shelter of the wall unit that housed my 27-inch television. There, safely barricaded by the furniture fortress, she continued her histrionics. She would emerge from her techno-lair only after the offending child was gone.

I never understood Amanda's fear of small people; it was completely irrational. She hadn't been tortured or abused by a child. She loved me, my parents, my friends, her catsitters, and even visiting cable repairmen and plumbers, in whose toolboxes she liked to nap. In addition, both of my male cats were child-friendly to the point of enduring all sorts of tail-pulling and overstimulation in their bid to get attention and treats from two-legged beasts of all ages.

It's not that Amanda always rejected children out of hand. From time to time, she made attempts to face down her fears. Once, when I was babysitting a friend's infant at my apartment, Amanda came and sat at the edge of the chaise longue where the baby was napping. She appeared to be watching over the child and guarding her. Then something kicked in, and she realized that she was sharing a chair with a baby. In a flash, she ran behind the television, moaning and quaking with fear.

No, Amanda made it clear that children were not welcome in our home. That's why the presence of Sophia, a toddler who came over every day, didn't help matters. Sophia made fast friends with our cat Smokey and she lavished love on him while Amanda watched with jealousy from a safe distance. When Amanda could take no more of Sophia's presence, she would fly for cover in her usual refuge.

When Sophia was two years old, Smokey died after a brief illness. Sophia continued to visit, hoping that Amanda would take Smokey's place as her kitty friend. But Amanda would have none of this idea, and Sophia's feelings were hurt. "Amanda doesn't like me," Sophia would say mournfully.

"It's not that she doesn't like you," I'd say, lying. "She's just a scaredy-cat around kids. She'll love you when you get a little bigger."

Amanda did come around a little bit. She probably realized what she was missing. Gradually, Amanda was able to stay in the room for increasing periods of time when Sophia came to visit. Whenever Sophia wanted to play on my bed, Amanda would follow us into the bedroom and even sit on the bed, as long as she could hide behind me while Sophia sat on my other side. Still, if things got too loud or frisky or Sophia came too close, Amanda flew out of the room like a flash.

I didn't know it, but all that year Amanda had mammary cancer. By the time her illness became obvious, the cancer had advanced, and we realized that she would not survive. I'm convinced that Amanda also knew she was dying.

About two weeks before Amanda died, Sophia and her mother, Tami, visited us — ostensibly to say good-bye to Amanda. No sooner had they walked through our front door than Amanda left

the couch where she had been spending most of her time since becoming very ill. Slowly and laboriously, she made her way toward Sophia, even though it was clearly hard for her both physically and emotionally. Then Amanda did something she had never done before: She walked right up to three-year-old Sophia and offered her the top of her head to pet.

Carol's Amanda and Smokey

Sophia stood there looking at Amanda, not quite knowing what to do. By this time, Tami and I were crying. "Go ahead, Sophia, pet Amanda," we told her. "She wants you to. It's okay." Sophia reached out a tentative little hand and began to stroke Amanda. Even though she trembled, Amanda let Sophia touch her.

After that day, little Sophia continued to visit Amanda. Even in her final hours, Amanda would purr and raise her head in greeting, the better to experience the child's caresses.

Amanda eventually passed away. She chose a spot behind the chaise for her deathbed. But I was always inspired by the way my long-conflicted kitty, at the end of her life, did what many people cannot do: She made sincere and lasting amends. In essence, Amanda humbled herself and admitted that she had been wrong about Sophia. In doing so, she became a great teacher to those of us who are fortunate enough to have known her.

Meditation

Is there a Divine messenger in a feline body who has a message for you about facing your fears? Does someone need your forgiveness so that both of you can find peace of mind?

Nurse Melanie

Julie Ann Mock
Santa Barbara, California

"Sorry, Melanie, you can't come in here." It was August of 1993. I was hot, tired, and exasperated, but that meant nothing to my little black cat, who was determined to get into the bathroom. I was trying to feed and medicate a desperately ill cat whom I'd brought home from the shelter where I volunteer. Malnourished and unable to stand, Laska was close to death. Intensive care at home was a last-ditch effort to save her life.

"Melanie! Give it up! Go play with Alf." Alf, a Norwegian forest cat and Melanie's best friend, was always up for a game.

What is it about cats and closed doors? Even though Laska's illness wasn't contagious, it seemed to me that the last thing she needed was a visit from Melanie, my feline Welcome Wagon. Laska was so fragile, and she'd had such a hard time at the shelter. Why complicate and maybe even worsen the situation?

"Oh, all right, you can say hello if Laska doesn't mind. But just for one minute."

Holding my breath, and ready to grab Melanie at the first hint of trouble, I let her into the bathroom. I was amazed by what happened next.

"Prrrr," said Laska, bowing her head in deference. Melanie said nothing. She simply went to work, grooming the sick cat with great tenderness and enthusiasm. Feeling the rough tongue on her forehead, Laska closed her eyes with obvious pleasure. She extended her neck for more of Melanie's TLC.

Melanie's spa treatments continued several times a day for many weeks until Laska was able to keep herself clean. These days, the two girls engage in equal-opportunity grooming. In August of 2000, we celebrated seven years with Laska, who has filled out to be a slender

Julie's Melanie and Laska

but gorgeous tortie-with-white charmer with sparkling green eyes. We owe all of those seven years to Melanie, the little black angel cat who wouldn't let a closed door stop her from helping a friend heal.

Meditation

Sometimes those who need us the most close the door to being helped. How persistent are you at offering your aid to someone who only appears to not want or need it?

The Presence of Willie

Judith A. Morris

Key Largo, Florida

*W*hen I was diagnosed with cancer of the breast, I decided after much consideration to go for totally alternative treatment. While struggling to survive, I initially felt a little frightened because of the stigma of death that is automatically attached to the word *cancer*. I felt alone, abandoned, and unsure of myself because I was stepping out on my own, choosing not to use traditional cancer therapy. Even though I am a nurse and a researcher, medical personnel I knew did not approve of my decision. My doctor swore that I would die if I didn't follow his prescribed treatment. Even so, I felt determined to research alternative methods. I came across Dr. Royal Rife's Light and Sound treatment, and my instincts told me that this alternative approach was the right one for me. My husband agreed, but we were alone in our decision — that is, until a special cat came into our lives.

Around the same time when I was facing cancer, a dear neighbor passed over from cancer after using traditional treatment, and she left her cat Willie to me. Willie had been a feral kitten. His type of cat is likely to be recognized as a breed someday, but for now it is known as a Keys cat or mangrove cat. Keys cats are usually gray-striped, with dark, leopardlike spots. In addition to having this typical coloring, Willie was long, lanky, and bowlegged. His tail seemed way too long for his body, and his large, yellow-green eyes peered out from an apple-shaped head. Willie's vocalizing sounded like squeaking. He loved to climb, and he always lived in the moment. Willie was a fellow who just seemed to have a love for life.

With the treatment modalities I was using, I had to lie down on my bed for a while each day. It was a complete surprise when, soon after we had adopted Willie, he began to join me while I administered the treatments to myself. He would jump up on my bed and walk the length of my body, starting at my feet and moving upward until he stood near my face and stared with his very large eyes into my eyes. He would then stretch his body out along my side and massage my cancerous breast with his paws!

Judith's Willie

The first two times Willie did this, I moved him to my other side. Each time, he insisted on returning to his position and massaging my afflicted breast tissue. As he did this, I saw deep love and compassion in his eyes. From that day on, Willie would stay with me, continuing his massage after each treatment session.

At first, when Willie massaged my breast, I cried with a release of sorrow at the realization that God truly knew and cared about me and was showing love through this gentle, sweet cat. Over time, I came to accept Willie's way of helping me heal without question or concern. Each time we went through our special routine, I smiled gratefully at him.

Today I am doing well, and tests show that my cancer is in

remission. How could I not be better after the Light and Sound treatments — and, of course, the Divine help from a cat healer?

Meditation

Are there additions to or alternatives for healing that you may be overlooking? Has a cat ever increased your courage to try the unconventional? Has a cat's persistence taught you to receive love and healing, no matter what form it comes in?

The Kinky Cat Who Chose Me

Graceann Maciolek
Milwaukee, Wisconsin

By the time I turned seventeen, I had wanted my own cat for a long time. Finally, I managed to wear down my parents' resistance. We went to the Humane Society and headed into the drab, depressing rooms full of cages. Cats and kittens were all around, mewing and sleeping and vying for attention. Of course, I wanted to take all of them home.

My mother was looking at a litter of Persian kittens who were barely eight weeks old, and I was watching her coo to them when I felt something tap me on the shoulder. I turned to find a scrawny little tabby cat, who appeared to be about four months old, reaching his paw out of the cage. He was all big head and feet. When I looked at him, he gave a lusty meow and pawed at me again.

I fell instantly and deeply in love. I said to my mother, "I want this homely kitty with the big head!"

As I inspected him further, I realized that this kitty had a crooked tail; it appeared to have been slammed in a door. This imperfection only made me love him more. He was all alone in the world, just like I felt at the time, and we had found each other. I had been terribly lonely, and often felt depressed; my high-school sweetheart had recently dumped me unceremoniously on my birthday.

I was by far the youngest child in my family, and there was nobody close to my age to confide in.

I hurried to find an attendant to get Kinky (as I had already named him) out of that horrible cage. I could hardly wait to hold him in my arms. Mom protested loudly about how homely and goofy the kitten looked, but I could not be swayed. By touching my shoulder, Kinky had chosen me. How could I refuse the honor?

When I took Kinky out of the cage and handed him to Mom, he crawled up on her chest and licked her cheek. Obviously, he had chosen her, too! She turned to me and said, "Oh, all right." From that moment on, I had my very own little fur-baby to love.

Graceann's Kinky

Kinky grew into a beautiful, healthy, substantial cat and an irrepressible lap fungus. He and I shared our lives through ten years of my ups and downs. Kinky was there for me no matter what was going on: divorce, illness, even the death of loved ones. I could always count on Kinky to comfort me. My lap was never empty, and whenever I curled up in a ball on my bed to cry, Kinky cuddled under my chin and let me soak his stripes with my tears. His purr was like a lullaby to me, and he was always willing to share it. It never mattered to him when I gained weight or if I had to start my adult life all over by moving into a tiny apartment after owning a lovely house. As long as we were together, Kinky was happy. And that, in turn, made me happy.

In the summer of 1995, Kinky started slowly but steadily losing weight and having trouble keeping his meals down. When I took him to the vet for diagnosis, a tumor was discovered in his stomach. During exploratory surgery, my vet found that my little Kinky kitty's body was riddled with cancer and that he must have been hurting for quite some time prior to the outward appearance of his symptoms. Based on what the vet found, I gave my consent for Kinky to be sent to the Rainbow Bridge on September 26, 1995, without waking him from surgery. The Rainbow Bridge is the legendary place where our beloved pets are said to go after death — and to someday be reunited with us. When we arrive there, we will cross the Rainbow Bridge together and never be parted again.

When I lost Kinky, it hurt me more than I can describe. How do you soothe your grief when a cat chose you, and the chooser goes ahead to wait for you? I am comforted to know that Kinky is no longer in pain, but every day I miss him terribly.

When I leave this world for the next, I hope to hear Saint Peter say, "Your mother has been waiting for you, Grace. And she's holding a tabby cat with a crooked tail."

Meditation

Has a cat helped you overcome loneliness? What did the cat do to let you know that you had not been abandoned? How could you give this kind of reassurance to someone else?

A Loyal Friend until the End

Ms. Anastasia Lynn Baima, A.S.
Woodbridge, Virginia

*M*ommas is a gray tabby with beautiful tiger striping. When we found her, she was pregnant and had been abused — left to fend for herself and have her kittens on the street. I was in my first year of college when my parents took in Mommas and Persephone, the stray cat's one remaining baby. We were grateful for their presence. Thorndike, our cat of fifteen years, had recently died. Our grief over losing him was great, and we didn't want to continue living in a catless home. We needed what I call "furry love," especially because I was the only child living at home after my two older sisters had moved out. To our good fortune, Mommas and her daughter proved to be experts in the field of cat psychology; they knew how to take care of people's emotional needs.

Mommas earned her name by adopting my parents and me as if we were her brood. Shortly after coming home with us, Mommas began following us around to see what we were up to. Whenever any of us cried, Mommas sat at our feet and waited patiently until she could administer her love and comfort.

After years of living in the same town, my parents moved to Pennsylvania with Mommas and Persephone, while my sisters and I stayed behind in Massachusetts. My father meant everything to me, and the last thing I would ever have wanted was for him to die alone. Yet one night, my worst fears seemed to have come true. My sisters arrived at my doorstep with some very sad news: Our mother had called to tell them that she'd come home to find my father lying on the living room floor; he had passed away while watching television. To my relief, though, my sisters said that my father had not been alone in the last moments of his life. A very dear friend had been with him: Mommas.

Anastasia's Mommas

Mommas had been my father's constant companion when my mother traveled for her job. The night that she found him in an everlasting sleep, she also found Mommas sitting by his side. Even as my mother cried over him, this cat would not leave my father. When the ambulance came, Mommas paced back and forth and dug her claws into the carpet at any attempt to make her move. Finally, my mother coaxed her into the bedroom so that attendants could take my father's body away.

After my father's death, Mommas tended to my mother day and night, through all the hard times. She made the house seem less lonely. With her attentiveness, Mommas helped ease the painful memories. Whenever my mother or I cried, Mommas patiently sat next to us, lifted a paw to touch our arm or hand, and licked the tears from our faces to let us know she was near. She stayed very quiet so as not to disturb us; she seemed to know that we needed to grieve. After we stopped crying, Mommas would begin the loudest, most warming purr. Then she'd climb onto one of our laps. I don't know how my mother and I would have gotten through those times without Mommas.

Almost a year after my father's death, Mommas became ill with hyperthyroidism. Without expensive cancer treatment and medicine, she might have died. We did not hesitate to care for her. We couldn't lose her now. After all, she was a member of our family. As she began to shed pound after pound, we worked endlessly with Mommas to make sure she ate extra food to keep her weight up. Eventually, she shrank from her normal twelve-pound figure to a small seven pounds. When we decided to take her to a vet for radiation treatment, the staff told us they'd never seen a cat like Mommas; she was in better health than other patients at this weight. On the day of her treatment, Mommas clung to all the vet technicians, purring and letting them cuddle her.

I am grateful to say that Mommas returned to good health. Unfortunately, we lost Persephone to diabetes and old age this year. It is strange to watch Mommas hold on gracefully as so many pass away before her. She is now the head of a household that includes two large dogs we took in from the streets. We also now have Dutchess, a young new cat who was abused and neglected. Dutchess watches Mommas's every move, learning how to act, where to go, and what to eat.

Mommas has aged a lot. She is much thinner now, and her hair has lost most of its luster. She is quiet and content to sit in the sun while grooming her fur. Even though I know my time with her is limited, I try not to think about it. Instead, I focus on what Mommas has taught me. I have learned more from this cat about unconditional love, respect, and family responsibility than from anyone else. Hers is a love that no words can adequately describe. Above all else, Mommas is the reason I have become a veterinary technologist. She inspired me with a passion that I take seriously and hold dear. I am learning to care for those who do not speak of their suffering, who quietly tend to us and ask only for our love in return.

Meditation

The loyalty of a true friend can be one of the greatest comforts in life. Are there others, animal or human, who are hurting and need you by their side?

Lil Mama and Her Kittens

Patty Hall Laswick
Shippenville, Pennsylvania

*A*fter several surgeries and a year and a half of quality life after his diagnosis, I lost my beloved cat Joey to cancer. He was euthanized on November 27, 1995. I grieved long and hard for him. On the eve of the first anniversary of Joey's death — a time when missing him overwhelmed me with great sadness and a sense of loss — I went to the front door to feed a stray cat. This cat had been coming to my porch for three years. No matter how I coaxed him, though, he would not come inside that whole time. But this evening, I noticed that the stray was waiting cautiously near the porch.

I wondered why he was so hesitant. Then, lo and behold, I saw the reason: A mother calico cat and her two little kittens emerged from the rhododendrons and onto the porch. In a procession, one gray-and-white kitty (whom I named Einstein) came first and growled at my regular stray cat (now called Tom). Einstein clambered onto the food bowl and helped himself. Then the calico cat (now known as Lil Mama) and her black-and-tan tabby kitten (Bohr) began to eat, too. Tom, gentleman that he was, allowed them to finish what would have been his meal.

After hearing about the cat family, some animal-loving friends of mine built a shelter on my porch and filled it with straw for the new arrivals. Since the weather was getting raw and cold, and the kitty family refused to come inside, this shelter kept the mother and her babies warm for the next six weeks. All that time, Tom continued to drop by regularly for his feeding, but he never ate the family's food or tried to take over their shelter. He would just scamper off into the night when he finished his meal.

Patty's Lil Mama

At that point, the weather became especially cold, so I opened my front door a crack. Before then, the two kittens would sometimes dart inside the house, but they always hurried outside as soon as I made a move to shut the door. This cold night, though, they stayed inside as I gently closed the front storm door.

I went back outdoors and sat on the porch. When Lil Mama approached me, I scooped her up in my arms and brought her safely inside, then closed the inside door. She leaped five feet in the air, trying to get out. That night, she urinated and defecated on my rug. She hid behind the washing machine, loudly meowing to express her unhappiness. Her two kittens, however, immediately started using the litter boxes I provided for them.

The kittens have now become happy adult cats. Lil Mama is also a contented, grateful middle-aged lady. The first stray, Tom, decided that being adopted by me might be a good idea after all, and he moved inside to join our family.

I am convinced that, on the anniversary of Joey's death, when I grieved so hard for him, Lil Mama brought her family to my porch — not by accident or coincidence, but by Divine design. I will always dearly love and miss my baby Joey, but I have been able to expand that love and joyfully open my heart with the help of the other feline companions who came to fill it.

Meditation

When has God, or the Divine, brought a creature into your life who helped you forget your losses and ease your pain?

Ask Cuddles

Dear Cuddles,

Why were cats given such amazing powers to heal
with their purrs, their companionship, and their
unconditional love?

Sincerely,
A Cat Purr-son

Dear Cat Purr-son,

We cats are endowed with healing powers because we
don't hesitate to use them, even if no one notices.

Intriguingly yours,
Cuddles

What can heal more deeply than laughter? And who has lived with cats without being amused by these tender little playmates? The next chapter will introduce you to the world of cat humor and feline fun. Read it with joy.

CHAPTER THREE

Were We Meant to Play with Our Littermates?

"All right," said the Cat; and this time it vanished quite slowly,
beginning with the end of the tail and ending with the grin,
which remained some time after the rest of it had gone.

— Lewis Carroll, *Alice's Adventures in Wonderland*

Cuddles's favorite game with us is hide-and-seek. She tucks herself under the bedcovers, forms a lump that she pretends we can't see, and stealthily waits there. Meanwhile, we call her name — "Cuddles, Cuddles, where are you?" — while searching under the bed, in the closet, and behind the nightstands. After a few minutes of this game, she slithers out, pokes her head up, and gives a look that says, "You are the worst hunters in the world!"

Cats know how to take the lighter touch. They experience life from an entirely different point of view than humans or any other animals do. Witness the humble objects a cat's imagination can transform into playthings: bottle caps, Q-tips, paper clips, pencils, or anything that rolls.

That wonderful wit known as Anonymous or Author Unknown has penned several short pieces that peek into a cat's clever and resourceful mind. These float around the Internet for the sole purpose of letting cat lovers commiserate and laugh with one another. We'd like to share a few with you.

There was some sort of gathering of their accomplices. I was placed in solitary throughout the event. However, I could hear the noise and smell the foul odor of the glass tubes they call "beer." More importantly, I overheard that my confinement was due to MY power of "allergies." Must learn what this is and how to use it to my advantage.

Grace personified,
I leap into the window.
I meant to do that.

Play: This is very important. Get enough sleep in the daytime so you are fresh for playing Catch Mouse or King of the Hill on your human's bed between 2:00 and 4:00 A.M.

Because cats are such masters at play, they are also wonderful with children. Dr. Marty Becker writes in *The Healing Power of Pets:* "Children who help raise animals are better at decoding body language and understanding others' feelings and motives — what psychologists call 'empathy.'"[1] Having pets apparently teaches children even more than compassion and altruism. In his article "What Pets Teach Kids," W. Bradford Swift, D.V.M., reports on a survey of Fortune 500 executives that appeared in *The Wall Street Journal.* The study indicated that 94 percent of the business leaders had pets while growing up. Swift says, "Many of the executives said their pets had taught them responsibility, empathy, and sharing, as well as providing valuable companionship."[2]

Companionship is one of the most wonderful gifts a cat offers to a child or an adult. Friendship with a cat may mean being invited to catch a rare glimpse of the feline worldview. The stories told in this chapter will also give you marvelous insights into life in cat-land.

One of the accounts is from former major-league baseball player Brian McRae, who hosts *Major League Baseball Radio* and has been a guest commentator on *Tonight on ESPN.* Brian batted .261 during his ten seasons in the majors, playing with teams in Kansas City, Chicago, and New York. In 1995, he finished fourth in the American League in hits. In 1998, prior to retiring from his ten seasons as an outfielder, Brian had his best year in the National League: He slugged twenty-one home runs and drove seventy-nine RBIs with a .264 average. Sounds like a guy who knows how to play, doesn't he? Yet Brian admitted to us that it took two little cats to teach him the true value of play.

Major-League Assistance from "the Sisters"

Brian McRae
Kansas City, Kansas

"The Sisters" arrived in my home when they were only a few weeks old. I had never considered myself a cat person, but a little dark-brown, tiger-striped kitten named Monster and her black, shorthaired sister, O-fer, have turned out to be two of my best buddies. They saw me through the highs and lows of playing major-league baseball in ways I would have never thought possible.

Golfers name their pets Birdie and Bogie, so I wanted to give one of these sisters a baseball name. I decided to call the kitten with the most outgoing personality O-fer. "O" (meaning zero) is used in phrases like "o for 1" or "o for 2" — a way of indicating how many times a player has been up to bat without hitting the ball into the field. This isn't the kind of record a baseball player wants to have by the end of a game, but as it turned out, O-fer was a good name for a cat who helped me get through some tough times.

Monster got her name because, as a kitten, she tore up everything in sight. From an early age, she scratched more than O-fer did and was more aggressive. She would chew on newspapers, shoes, or anything else she could reach. Even now, I have to be careful not to leave the bathroom door open, or Monster will unroll toilet paper, leaving a trail of scraps all over the house. I would love to set up a video camera just to see what these two are up to while I'm gone.

When Monster and O-fer first came to live with me, the kittens didn't do a whole lot. They spent most of their time sleeping, and they were kind of boring. After about a week, they got adjusted, started running around the house, and became more interesting. They began to play games by hiding behind dressers or curling up together in one of the bottom drawers, where I would eventually find them.

I have to admit that, because I have no children, Monster and O-fer are like kids to me. I give them bottled water to drink. When I open the refrigerator, they are right there, waiting for me to feed them leftovers. They follow me around the house and sleep in my bed at night. I enjoy hanging out with the cats, playing with them for as much as a couple of hours at a time. They bring their toys to me and insist that it's playtime.

You might think that my cats' favorite toys would be the ones I buy for them, but Monster and O-fer don't play with anything conventional. Their favorite playthings are multicolored straws, shoe-strings, and the plastic ring from a milk bottle. I used to spend lots of money on toys, but these two cats always found something around the house they wanted to play with more.

Monster and O-fer love it when I put them out on my gated balcony, where they can soak up sunshine, watch birds fly by, and listen to the chirping. As independent-minded creatures full of attitude, these sister cats keep me amused.

In 1997, when I played center field for the Chicago Cubs, my wife and I decided to take Monster and O-fer to Chicago with us.

Because playing baseball is great when your team is winning and not so great when you're losing, the decision to bring "the Sisters" along turned out to be one of the best I ever made during my professional career. By mid-April, the Cubs were at 0 for 14. Basically, the season was over for us. But we still had many more ball games to play and a lot of disappointed fans to face. After each game, I'd return home to

Brian's O-fer

find Monster and O-fer waiting for me. What a relief they provided from the stress of the day or week!

Unlike other major-league sports, in which there's time off between games, just about every day is a play day in baseball; we don't have days off. A baseball team starts playing in March and continues through October. At the most, ballplayers have maybe 7 to 10 days off out of 170 to 180 days of playing. So we have the pressure of performing every day.

Time away from the game allows a player to put his mind on other things. But because we play baseball every day, one day bleeds into the next. It's like we're spending one endless day going through grinding routines, over and over again. We may be in a different city or playing against a different team, but it all seems pretty much the same. Sometimes it's as if the day never stops.

Many of the stresses and pressures that come up in a baseball season are due to traveling a lot. We spend half our time on the road. Major-league baseball is a mentally grueling sport because we must live out of a suitcase. A ballplayer might be in New York one day, Los

Angeles the next day, and Oakland the next day, but he is still expected to play well each day.

Because of the lack of days off and the amount of travel, a baseball player must be able to relax and regroup mentally. If you've had a bad day, you need to really shake it off, because the next day you must go out there and perform again. If you dwell on your losses, it's easy to let a bad day or two turn into a bad week. During the season, you get caught up in whether your team is playing well or not. You wonder if you're personally doing all you can do to help the team win.

Although my teammates and I were spiraling downward during the 1997 season, Monster and O-fer had no clue what I did for a living or what was going on in my time away from them. As far as they were concerned, my purpose in life was to play with them and be happy. Rolling around on the floor with Monster and O-fer put the outside world and its pressures into perspective for me. I'd find myself thinking, "Why worry?" Spending time with the cats helped me focus on what is important in the grand scheme of things. I was grateful for the gift of enjoyment with companions who didn't care what I did for a living. Monster and O-fer didn't know if I'd had a good or bad game; it simply didn't matter to them what I did at the ballpark.

Being with Monster and O-fer in Chicago reminded me that I didn't need to be upset about a bad game. After all, how could I be angry after lying on the floor with two cats rolling around on top of me, tugging at my ears, and licking my fingers? When I came home from a game, I threw straws and milk rings, and they ran and brought these favorite toys back to me. I relaxed by brushing and grooming the cats and clipping their back claws. When they were younger, it had been a big ordeal to bathe them. But as they got older, the cats learned to like playing with water, and they enjoyed splashing it from the sink. Whenever I took a bath, they liked to sit on the edge of the bathtub and poke their paws in my bathwater.

Playing with Monster and O-fer caused me to realize that I could get joy from things besides baseball. Even when something didn't go my way at work, the cats made me happy. They didn't ask questions; they didn't pass judgment. Their companionship allowed me to separate work from home.

Lots of ballplayers can't do that. If they have one bad day, it leads to two bad days, then to three, and finally to an entire bad week. The game consumes them. Monster and O-fer were a good diversion for me. I often thought that if other ballplayers had buddies like these two cats, they would have an easier time handling the ups and downs of baseball. Have you noticed that you hardly ever see people in a bad mood when they're out walking their dogs?

Even though Monster and O-fer get mad and ignore me when I've been away for a while, they seem to know when I need attention, and they're more than willing to give it to me. If they see me resting on the couch, they can tell if I'm not feeling well. Then they come up and quietly lie on my lap. It's one of the most comforting feelings in the world.

Many changes occur in baseball and in life, but one thing I can count on is that Monster and O-fer are always there for me.

Meditation

What have cats taught you about the importance of play as a stress-reliever and mood-lightener? Is playtime a missing element in your life?

Muse of Mirth

Kevin Cole
New Bern, North Carolina

*L*ife with Alexander the Cat is an odyssey of amusement. (Spelled "a-*muse*-ment.")

Without noticeable effort, Alex draws open an unseen curtain across the stage of our lives, revealing bountiful orchards ripe with lighthearted inspirations. As professional writers, our responsibility is simply to catch the falling harvest. This means we keep our fruit-collecting basket handy all the time, because our muse of feline-driven creativity ("felinivity") could pounce at any moment. My wife, Patti, and I call him our resident Muse of Mirth.

We never know when Alex will work his sly, mirthful magic on our household — we're never certain that he actually *will* do so again. But whenever we decide that Alex's apparent magic is a fluke (although a curiously *recurring* fluke), he does something that brings a grin to our hearts. That, in turn, infuses us with creative energy to put pen to paper and help others see a mundane event in a different way. When that happens, we know our boy is weaving felinivity again.

Take the business with the ironing board, for example. Our ironing board stays up in the great room most of the time. It didn't start out that way. It started like the ironing board in everyone else's house: set up while in use, folded and stashed behind a door when not in use. A year or so ago, however, while doing a weeklong marathon of laundry and ironing, we left the ironing board set up.

During our brief window of domestic efficiency, Alexander made his move. Our resident muse of creativity and mirth laid claim to the ironing board as a safety plateau. It was one of the few places in the house where his occasional nemesis, Zak the Cat, seemed dis-inclined to pursue him. So, within a matter of days, Alex adopted the habit of eating and napping on top of the ironing board. Neither Patti nor I had the heart to dislodge him.

We lashed the ironing board to the great-room wall with wire and pushpins. Although Alex mounted the ironing board with graceful feline ease, his dismounts were a different story; when he shoved off, he created an equal-but-opposite reaction. The board would bang against the wall, rebound, and fall over with a clatter,

Kevin's Alexander

lying there like some fragile yard decoration blown over by wind. Our fear was that the falling board would one day injure one of the several other animals who call our house home. After we secured it bow and stern with wire and pushpins, the ironing board became as solid as the Rock of Gibraltar.

However, our efforts to placate Alex did not enhance the aes-thetics of our home. So we declared the ironing board to be art. First-time visitors to our house were impressed by this objet d'art.

Imagine the fifty-cent tour of our great room: "Over the fireplace you'll see Edward Robert Hughes's *Midsummer Eve,* one of his Victorian Faeries series. And on this wall is one of Patti's early works featuring...uh, we call it *Early Twenty-First-Century Ironing Board as Art, with Napping Tabby.* ...Yes, the realism is incredible, isn't it? From the artist's dePaws period. You'd swear the cat's actually breathing....But let's move on to the guest bath...."

Alexander has a way of facilitating joy. His presence carries a pixie-dusting of mirth, manifesting as an antithesis to the dust-cloud perpetually accompanying the Pig-Pen character in Charles M. Schulz's *Peanuts* comic strip. The Alex-generated playfulness might not issue forth as immediate laughter or chuckles. More often than not, it is only in its aftermath that the residual impact of Alex's pixie dust illuminates the lighter side of life's events.

Meditation

What pixie dust are cats sprinkling in your home and life? How is a cat's creativity helping you find joy in the little things?

Living with a Dickens

Judith A. Morris
Key Largo, Florida

I have been most grateful to my tortoiseshell cat, Dickens, for sharing her life with me. She is now sixteen years young and has a beautiful coat that looks and feels like mink. It is said that cats of this unique coloration are almost always female and that they are very lucky. That has proven to be true, but I can't help thinking that I'm the lucky one to share my life with Dickens.

I found Dickens as a kitten on a friend's farm in Missouri. I was looking for a black-and-white cat as a companion and friend for my black-and-white adult tomcat, who lived with me in my city apartment. I was new to cats at that time and only beginning to learn that cats choose us.

My farmer friend invited me to sit on the ground as we called to a litter of kittens. Out from under the barn ran five pretty little black-and-white kittens. In the lead was a strange little brownish kitty. She came right over to me, but I was not interested in her. To make her choice clearer, she jumped into my carrying box and sat there. I distractedly picked her up and placed her outside the box. Again, she bounced into the box. Now she had my attention. She was giving me strong, intelligent eye contact that said, "I am so HAPPY to find YOU!"

In that moment, I fell in love. At first I named the kitten Daisy, but after living with her for a short time, I saw that she was instant trouble — always getting into things and causing upsets. After she got into the habit of climbing up the back of my bare legs while I yelped at the digging of her needlelike claws, I changed her name to Dickens. The name fit her then, and it is still working.

Not knowing the danger of introducing a kitten to a strange, mature tomcat, I brought Dickens home, opened the door, and put her on the floor. My male cat, Duffy, was sitting up in the middle of the floor facing us, and his big gray eyes took in this little being. Dickens pranced right up to Duffy and raised her little paw as high as she could lift it. Then she patted the top of his head. In cat language, she was saying, "I am the dominant one here!"

Duffy leaned back, staring ominously, and I began to feel nervous. Suddenly, with one big paw, he pushed Dickens down to the floor and began washing her all over with immense love. Until the day Duffy died, he and Dickens slept arm-in-arm as a loving couple. Still, he never stopped falling for her little tricks. Dickens loved to wrestle with her gentle giant, Duffy. She would sneak up on Duffy while he napped and launch herself onto his tail, then ride it while he tried to run away. Finally, as if dealing with an overly excited child, Duffy would grab Dickens with all four legs and pull her tightly against him until she tired of squirming. Then they would fall asleep together in that position.

Dickens had a lively sense of humor, and Duffy seemed to be incredibly naïve around her. Frequently, as the two cats indulged in rough play, Dickens would overstep the bounds Duffy had set. Duffy would let her know that she'd gone too far by smartly boxing her with a paw to her head. She then would cower before him and carefully edge up to softly groom his fur until he relaxed. As soon as Duffy was off guard again, bam! Dickens would bite his ear. This would launch the two playmates into tussling and playing again. But over the years, Duffy bore all of Dickens's shenanigans with steadfast loyalty.

Dickens also consistently shows me devotion, playfulness, and love. But most of all, she has proven to me that a soul is a soul whether it is inside an animal or a human body. Through Dickens, I have learned that each soul is a unique part of the essence of God.

Dickens and I formed a spiritual bond early on when she began to appear in my lively world of dreams. I have studied my dreams for years, and I know the reality of other worlds where I live lives beyond this physical one.

In one of our otherworldly existences together, I have come to accept the fact that Dickens absolutely loves doughnuts! Being a cat, she cannot eat doughnuts here, of course. As if to make up for this deprivation, she frequently meets my husband, Steve, in the dream state; on the inner planes, they blissfully go to doughnut shops and have their fill of goodies. Dickens always "tells" the waitress to hurry and bring her doughnuts right away.

After Duffy died — or, I might say, translated his existence to another, lighter form — he often met my husband and Dickens at their favorite doughnut shop. In these dreams, Duffy always ordered oatmeal instead of doughnuts. (Duffy no longer comes into our dreams these days, so we think he may be incarnating again.) I should mention that, at these doughnut-shop encounters, a wondrous guardian, or spiritual master, accompanies Steve, Dickens, and

Duffy. This has shown me that the soul is greatly valued, loved, and cared for by the heavenly forces, no matter what form we take.

As if to verify what Steve and I experienced with Dickens in dreams, one day when I came home, she led me into the kitchen and straight to a box of doughnuts that was lying in the middle of the floor. Dickens vocalized and stared into my eyes while I grinned. Obviously, she was telling me that "someone" (a serious doughnut lover, perhaps?) had knocked this box of doughnuts off the table and onto the floor. It was a cardboard-and-cellophane box that contained an assortment of wonderfully colored doughnuts, with their tempting, yeasty, sugary smell. The box had been battered mercilessly; "someone" had worked earnestly to open it, but to no avail.

Judith's Dickens

During the day, Dickens is a pleasurable companion. But bedtime has become one of my favorite times to spend with this cat. She loves to lie beside my head while I lie on my side. When we are head to head, she gently licks my eyelids, then my nose. After the licking is accomplished, she settles back to look intensely into my eyes. She raises her paw and places it on my face as if she is holding me, while continuing to stare deeply into my very being. I actually feel her love transferring into me. Of course, I melt and give my love back to her. These are special transcendent moments for both of us.

One night, Dickens was in her usual position, ready to sleep near my face, and I was in that state between sleep and wakefulness. Dickens stared into my eyes, patting and kneading my cheek with her paw. Summoning all the love she could muster, I heard her speak to me inside my heart and mind. I knew that this was a real and precious gift from her to me. I will never forget how caringly Dickens expressed her great love in words I could understand. She said, "Oh, Judy, I love you so much. I just love you so very much!" This experience was as real as when my husband speaks to me in English. I told her that I love her, too. I went to sleep that night basking in the love and warmth of a cat who lives up to her name, yet who fills my life with joy and laughter.

In case I've given the impression that Dickens is all sweetness and light, I have to say that she is also a fierce alarm clock. When she knows it's time for us to get up, she works first on Steve and then on me. We sometimes play dead just to see how far she'll go in her efforts to get us out of bed. Usually, she begins by tugging at Steve's beard with a front paw. Then she sticks her paw up his nose! If that fails to wake him, she comes over to my side of the bed and licks my eyelids open with her raspy tongue. She finishes by sinking her teeth into my long hair and pulling hard. That maneuver works every time!

Recently, our aging Dickens developed allergies to all commercial cat foods. We agonized as we tried various brands, but even the health-food-store brands didn't work for her. She would eat and then vomit. She also developed bloody diarrhea, and the vet told us that Dickens had gone into kidney failure. The end was near.

That night, I held Dickens and talked to her. I told her that we love her very, very much and that we'd done all we knew to assist her. I explained that it was up to her, as soul, to decide if it was time for her to leave her physical body. I promised that we would respect her wishes. However, if she wanted to live longer in this body, she would have to help us.

Later, I slept and dreamed. My husband also dreamed. The next morning, we each awakened from our dreams with ideas for a clear and complex food regimen for Dickens. As our dreams had instructed, we gathered organic squash baby food, organic rice, organic vegetable bouillon, and other ingredients. We carefully cooked the foods in olive oil, parsley, and lots of garlic, then fed the concoction to Dickens. I kid you not, she is still thriving on this food.

Where did we get the recipe? I believe it came to us from Dickens's guardian angel, who is also our guardian. You might say he is the family's angel! How else could we have come up with such a perfect food cure for this wonderful soul who graces our lives in her lovely, aging cat's body?

Meditation

Did a cat ever join you in your dreams? What did you learn with or about a cat in the dream state that you hadn't understood before? Have you met your cat's guardian angel?

This Candy Is Reserved for Cats

Sue Stange
Cuyahoga Falls, Ohio

I adopted Lucy from the animal shelter where I volunteer, hoping that she would be good company for my mother. Mom had been spending a lot of time alone since my father died. Lucy is a big, high-energy gray cat — possibly a Maine coon mix. She turned out to be a one-person cat, and a lot of fun. Lucy became both an angel and an entertainer for my mother.

My mother kept six cellophane-wrapped peppermint candies in an attractive ruby-colored dish on the coffee table in her living room. Soon the peppermints became Lucy's favorite toy.

Sue's Lucy

The game my mother and Lucy played went something like this: Mom threw the candies toward the ceiling, and Lucy leaped high to grab them in midair with her paws. Sometimes Lucy would bat at the falling candies, then chase them as they rolled on the floor. But she would never return them to my mother. When my mother had thrown all the candies, Lucy would stand and wait while Mom picked them up so that they could play again. After their game, Mom would place the peppermints back in the candy dish.

Whenever Lucy wanted Mom to throw candies for her, she went to the dish, sat in front of it, and stared at the candy. This would start another round of catch-the-candy.

Guests to our home never did understand why my mother didn't offer them the peppermint candy that looked so inviting.

Meditation

Has a cat taught you a favorite game? How well have the cats in your life trained you to play with them?

Bam Bam Helped Me Pack for My Vacation

Darby Davis
Anaheim, California

*B*am Bam, rescued from an animal shelter, is a four-year-old caramel-colored cat with a white face, belly, and paws and golden-brown eyes that can see right into a person's soul. Bam Bam and I have a little ritual that we carry out every morning before I go to work: He always brings me one of his "toys." Actually, it's one of those plastic strips that must be pulled off an orange-juice jug before you can open it. He loves these strips because they're lightweight and easy for him to pick up and toss around. He plays fetch with them like a dog!

Recently, I was preparing for a weekend trip to Mexico with some friends. As I got ready to leave, I put my purse, suitcase, and camera on the floor next to the door. Then I placed a plastic bag there with some bottled water and apples in it for the long bus trip.

I played with Bam Bam for a while, then got dressed and ate breakfast. Then I said good-bye to him and headed out to meet my friends. Later that day, as we rode to San Felipe, I reached into my plastic bag and found that Bam Bam had helped me pack for the trip: He had put his little yellow plastic toy in the bag for me. Now, you know how plastic bags collapse when you set them down. It must have taken some effort on Bam Bam's part to tuck his toy far

Darby's Bam Bam

enough into the bag so that I would not see it and it wouldn't fall out when I picked up the bag to leave.

I get a little teary-eyed when I think about how Bam Bam sent me off with his favorite toy and seemed to want me to have a good time. He certainly was with me for the entire trip. To this day, I still can't believe what he did!

Meditation

Has a cat ever made sure you had what you needed for a physical or spiritual journey? What toys have the cats in your life used to remind you to play and relax?

A Place at the Table

Jenny Carlson
Minneapolis, Minnesota

*M*y cat, Rico, is a brown-and-gray tabby with beautiful green eyes. He has his own chair, and he sits at the dinner table with my husband and me. Now, mind you, by the time we sit down to eat, Rico has already had his own dinner (times two), but he wants to share in our meal as well.

Rico loves bagels, but this is a cat who will try any food once. His favorite treat is the cookies my dad feeds him whenever he comes over. It really doesn't matter what kind of cookie my dad brings. Rico even likes fortune cookies, so whenever we have Chinese food I share a cookie with my cat.

Jenny's Rico

Eating with us at the table may not be the best thing for Rico, but he is a big cat in good health, and we don't overdo it on the sweets. We find it funny to watch Rico perched on his own little chair and enjoying dinner with his family.

Meditation

What are your cat's favorite foods? Have cats taught you how to make family time memorable?

Cat's Hair

Pamela V. Brown
Kapaa, Kauai, Hawaii

*O*ur late, beloved cat Scooby was quite a character; he routinely captured the hearts of professed "non-cat" people. Scooby was a tabby who resembled a Maine coon cat, and he had an amusing preference for human hair. If I slung him over my shoulder, he'd reach around my neck, grab my hair with his paw, and start purring and drooling. I had to be careful not to hug him before going out for the day, or else I'd have drool in my hair!

Scooby's penchant for hair became legendary within our family. Once my brother purchased a dark-brown, shoulder-length wig for Scooby at a swap meet, and the cat loved it. He'd knead the wig with his paws in the middle of the living room floor, blissfully purring and drooling. With an ecstatic look on his face, he was clearly in nirvana. He would commune with the wig for hours, and he loved to nap with it. When visitors walked into our home, the wig on the floor certainly made for an interesting sight and required a quick explanation.

Scooby was definitely into brunettes. My husband and I both have dark hair, so that's the only hair color he ever knew at home. When my best friend, who has blond hair, visited us and picked up Scooby, the cat was thrown for a loop. He actually shied away from

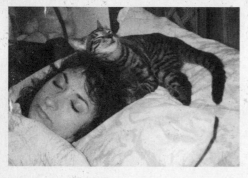

Pamela and Scooby

my friend's ponytail — something he never did with dark hair. We could tell that he wasn't sure what that straw-colored stuff was or what he was supposed to do with it. We all had a chuckle at his puzzlement.

Scooby was one of the most special cats my family ever had. We tell many funny stories about him, and we have wonderful photos and memories of Scooby sleeping on my hair and drooling into it.

Meditation

Have visitors to your home been met by cat surprises? Are there dimensions to your life, especially humorous ones, that only a cat could create?

Ask Cuddles

Dear Cuddles,

Why do people think cats are so funny?

Sincerely,
My Cat's Favorite Toy

Dear Favorite Toy,

We aren't nearly as funny as people. Unlike cats, when humans chase or roll around or stretch, they're trying to lose weight or get limber. Poor things, they're so amusing when they huff and puff like that. And, instead of a good licking, people require smelly soap and sloppy water for their baths! How weird is that?

Engagingly yours,
Cuddles

Okay, you can put the toys back in their basket. Now it's time to pull out your mirror. The next chapter will introduce you to the idea that the cat you chose (and/or who chose you) is in your life for a Divine purpose. Cats may be revealing more juice about you than your most gossipy friends.

CHAPTER FOUR

Are Cats Mirrors
of the Soul?

Tell me whom you love, and I'll tell you who you are.

— African-American folk saying

*I*n a radio interview we did for a provincewide station in Saskatchewan, Canada, a man named Van called in to tell us about his family's cat, Smokey. Van said that every time a family member has a problem or is in any kind of distress, Smokey reflects the distressing situation by sitting or sleeping on that person's bed.

Although Van realizes, in retrospect, that the cat has been doing this for years, he never noticed Smokey's behavior until his daughter went away to college. One night, Smokey slept on Van's daughter's bed, looking very morose. Seeing Smokey there made Van miss his daughter, so he called her at her dormitory to chat. That's when he learned that she'd been admitted to the hospital that day, very sick with the flu. Not wanting to alarm her family, she hadn't called. Although he lived many miles away from the girl, Smokey had delivered the message.

Now the family has learned to recognize Smokey's signal. If they see him on a family member's bed, Van calls to ask if there is trouble. Smokey has never been wrong about his diagnosis of a family member's condition. When all is well with everyone, Smokey peacefully sleeps on the couch in the living room.

Smokey serves as this family's mirror. Many cats do something similar, although not usually as dramatically as Smokey does. Cats often take on the characteristics and even the problems of their human family members. They generously ignore the wisdom in Mark Twain's observation: "If a man could be crossed with a cat, it would improve the man but it would deteriorate the cat."[1]

Conversely, people choose to live with cats who reflect their personalities, philosophies, and spiritual aspirations. In Don Holt's book *Praying with Katie: God, My Cat, and Me,* this retired pastor and lay minister writes of his cat, "[Katie] set me wondering. Might I not be able to love God in the ways that Katie was loving me? A desire to be close, to be in touch, to receive strokes and caresses from the Eternal, to feel warm and safe and comfortable with God? Was this not exactly what I longed for — the experience of stretching out, so to speak, on the breast of God, purring in contentment, safely supported by the everlasting arms?"[2]

The stories in this chapter tell remarkable tales of cats who seem to have wandered into people's lives in the most startling displays of synchronicity. Often the cats' experiences parallel those of their human companions.

As you'll see in this chapter, cats — gazing into our faces with unconditional love — hold up the mirror of self-awareness with un-flinching honesty.

My Patient and My Healer

Laurie Crawford Stone
Cedar Rapids, Iowa

I adopted my cat Teddy from a shelter on Valentine's Day 1997. I had been in the process of adopting two other cats at the shelter, while Teddy napped unaware. But as I began to leave, Teddy awakened, stretched, and slowly looked me directly in the eye. That look said it all; this cat knew he was supposed to come home with me.

Teddy was unique in both personality and appearance. He was the longest, tallest cat I have ever seen. Our shortest cat could walk underneath him. Teddy had a magnificent twelve-inch tail. A white handlebar moustache, white chest and paws, and white racing stripes on his legs accentuated his gray fur. He was a perfect blend of beauty and masculinity. Teddy had a habit that always amused and touched me: He would bring a toy ball to the entrance of the room where I was working or sleeping, then lie there patiently waiting for me to play. If I left the room and found a ball by the entrance, I knew Teddy had been there.

During his monthlong stay at the shelter, Teddy had shown the temperament to become a therapy cat. The shelter volunteers often took him out to visit nursing-home residents, who must have loved his easy ways, his friendly face, and his tender touch.

After Teddy came to live with us, he continued to be a nurturing type of cat. When our cat Coco had a difficult recovery after being spayed, Teddy stayed by her on our bed for a month, rarely leaving her side.

Teddy was our ambassador; he greeted all visitors. He guarded the door of any room I used for fostering rabbits, cats, or dogs. He was always careful to help creatures who were in trouble. Seeing Teddy standing vigil by a closet door was a sure sign that one of our cats had been trapped inside.

But of all the creatures Teddy cared for, I was his most important project. Teddy and I both had health problems for several years, and some of our symptoms were remarkably similar.

At one point, Teddy developed breathing problems that made it impossible to play with him; he would become winded after one high jump. This was a sad situation for a cat who had previously been able to leap enthusiastically into the air, tirelessly play fetch with his toy balls, and race around the house for no apparent reason. Although his symptoms and diagnostic testing indicated asthma, he did not respond to asthma medications. We started keeping doors and windows closed except on a few nice days. I installed air filters in the bedroom and sun porch. We switched to all-natural cleaning products and purchased special vacuum cleaners. Visitors were asked to remove their shoes. Yet nothing we did seemed to help Teddy get better.

Around this time, I injured my shoulder and neck, making it impossible for me to participate in the exercise regimen that had been an important part of my daily life. I had been a gymnast as a child, and I remained active for years. It was devastating to be unable to lift even a bag of groceries. Teddy and I both had to restrict our physical activities in order to be comfortable. It felt so strange that the two of us were simultaneously limited from doing our normal activities. I could relate to how frustrating and frightening this must have been for Teddy. But at least I had an explanation for my changes and the opportunity to improve with therapy. We had no explanation for Teddy's symptoms, and we couldn't find anything that brought him relief.

Teddy also had irritable bowel syndrome, which required that I cook for him. We visited veterinary teaching colleges and consulted with specialists, but no one had seen problems like Teddy's. Diagnostic tests revealed nothing. The vets suspected that Teddy had allergies, but his symptoms didn't improve after allergy treatments. Teddy stumped the veterinarians.

Meanwhile, medical doctors were puzzled by my own combination of gastrointestinal symptoms, fatigue, and elevated liver enzymes. Since Teddy and I both had gastrointestinal problems, I installed a water purifier, thinking that something simple like the chemicals in the city water might be the culprits. Still, neither of us improved.

After I underwent a year of testing, doctors finally discovered that I had tumors throughout my liver. I was immediately scheduled for a biopsy. It appeared that I had metastasized liver cancer. Six weeks, three biopsies, and three hospitals later, I learned that the tumors were not malignant. That was the good news. The bad news was that I had a rare liver disease.

I felt as if I had been given a second chance, and I decided to make major changes in my life. I knew this was my opportunity to address the toll that work had been taking on my health. I vowed to spend more time with my cats and to better care for myself. I would set boundaries and change my work habits.

I am the cofounder and president of Animal Advocates of Iowa, a nonprofit animal advocacy group. The telephone line for Animal Advocates comes into my house, and I am the contact person named on our Website. This means that I can work whenever I want. It also means that people can contact me at all hours. Before my final biopsy, I arranged things so that people who contacted me could find answers to many routine animal questions on our Website.

I had a wonderful couple of months. I focused on doing what I love. I spent time every day playing with my cats. I began a new exercise program. I played music, I read, and I wrote. I took time for lunch and coffee with friends. I started doing a nightly healing meditation. I quit spending time with people who drained me. I stopped doing things that depleted me emotionally. I lived each day as if it might be my last. I maintained my boundaries in relation to my work. I learned to say no, and I felt for the first time in years that I was spending each day in the best way for me.

Gradually, as I started feeling better and stronger, I took on new projects. The work quickly mushroomed, and I was once again caught up in it. I was aware of the severe emotional strain this took on my health, but I seemed to be unwilling and unable to refuse the many requests for my help.

During the time when I was starting to work too much again, my beloved Teddy's health worsened. This change in his condition caused me to quit almost everything else I was doing to care for him. I focused on Teddy — and on me. At last I had a good reason to say no to people's requests, and I was able to establish much-needed boundaries to protect my own health.

Despite trips to veterinarians, extensive research, holistic treatments, consultations with animal communicators, and even DNA testing, Teddy continued to decline. He now had elevated liver enzymes, just as I did. No one could tell me what was wrong with him. I felt desperate and frantic. I could do nothing to protect, treat, or save my beloved companion. Like me, it appeared that Teddy had a rare disease.

As I continued to care for him, Teddy responded with great affection by comforting me during my times of fear, grief, and frustration. Teddy stayed wherever I was in the house. If I felt upset, he would come over and stroke my shoulder with his paw and look straight into my eyes as if to tell me things would be okay. At night, he always jumped onto the bed and settled his wonderful, solid body snugly against mine, often putting a paw on my leg. I believe he tried to keep our routine as normal as possible, and he continued to do things to make me laugh. Toward the end of his life, he even bounded up the stairs one last time. He always came to eat, since he knew that made me happy; even if he wasn't hungry, he would take little bites.

Laurie's Teddy

I was devastated when Teddy's beautiful body started growing visible tumors. An oncologist at the University of Wisconsin's Veterinary Medical Teaching Hospital suggested that the tumor in Teddy's eye might be the result of lung cancer, but a lung needle biopsy turned out negative. Needle biopsies of the skin tumors were also negative. The appearance of tumors narrowed Teddy's diagnosis to one of three diseases, none of which had a good prognosis.

Even though we treated Teddy for what we could, his condition worsened. It became apparent that I couldn't do anything more for him medically. I continued to tell him stories, sing to him, and sleep with him every night. I finally turned to my Higher Power and asked for guidance.

Forty-eight hours after my prayer, on March 16, 2003, Teddy began to have severe difficulty breathing. This time, there was no relief. He rested on the bed with his paws on my arm. Even in his last hours, Teddy comforted me as he passed from this earth and was finally free.

We learned from the necropsy, done within hours of Teddy's passing, that he had cancer everywhere in his body except his liver. The diagnosis was metastasized lung cancer — an extremely rare condition in cats. The doctors didn't know how Teddy could have kept breathing with his lungs so full of cancer.

They didn't understand, but I do.

Teddy couldn't leave until I finally realized that my will could no longer keep him here. For months, I had prayed for Teddy to be healed. I prayed for a diagnosis and treatment. Teddy was on prayer lists in several states. I really thought the power of prayer would heal him. Finally, I turned my will over to God and asked that *his* will be done. It was the first prayer in which I acknowledged that Teddy might not live.

I asked God if he would please let me know when it was time for Teddy to leave so that I could let him go. I then said the Serenity Prayer, which reminds us to accept the things we cannot change. I repeated the Serenity Prayer many times over the next two days. Although I knew that my will could not heal Teddy, when I finally acknowledged it, I believe that God was able to answer my prayer. When I turned my will over to God, I had a sense of peace. I knew that his will, not mine, would be done.

Later that year, after Teddy's passing, further medical testing revealed that all of my liver enzymes but one were back to normal. My liver is still riddled with tumors, but there is no evidence of malignancy or impaired function.

I still don't understand why Teddy had to die when he was only six years old. I don't understand why there were so many things wrong with him. Yet I look at his illness and death as gifts of life to me and our other cats. Teddy taught me how important relationships are and how much my other six cats love and need me. He taught me that I can't solve all the problems in the world and that I don't need to keep working so hard. Teddy didn't want to go, and I didn't want him to leave. But I am grateful that we had a blessed final four months together while I was his nurse and he was my healer.

I do not believe in coincidences. I believe in a God who works in mysterious ways. I believe that I was healed through Teddy. Teddy's liver remained untouched by cancer, while the rest of his body was wracked with malignant tumors. I don't know why Teddy's liver enzymes were elevated, and neither do the doctors. That is part of the mystery. How could his liver be okay when the rest of his body was filled with cancer, from his eyes to the very tip of his tail? If Teddy's liver could be healthy despite all of this cancer and our shared problem of elevated liver enzymes, then certainly my own liver — though riddled with currently benign tumors — can remain free of cancer. It's almost as if Teddy's liver belonged in my body, and my liver belonged in his. I believe that Teddy gave me this message of hope and healing by taking on the cancer in other parts of his body so that I could stay healthy. I believe that God worked through Teddy to renew my physical and spiritual life.

My life is different for having had Teddy in it. Teddy derived pleasure from everything. He loved life. Teddy gave me the special gift of his unconditional love. His connection to me on a spiritual level has led me to a renewed relationship with God. I now experience the wonder of the workings of God in my life. Since turning things with Teddy over to God, I have continued to surrender difficult situations. Each time I do this, God responds. I turned things over to God two days before my return visit to the doctor, and I received an immediate sense of peace. I knew I was going to have a good report.

Teddy continues to be a catalyst for miracles and blessings. After I e-mailed a draft of this story to Allen and Linda Anderson, I went to the grocery store. When I returned, I found one of Teddy's toy balls inside my back door. I used to find these balls outside the bedroom and the office — the two rooms where I spent most of my time. The balls were Teddy's signature that he'd been there. Yet he had never left a ball near the back door. That day, when I wrote his story for the first time, Teddy's ball was sitting in the middle of the rug, right where I wouldn't miss it. I felt that Teddy was sending me a message; he wanted to tell me that he, too, was thinking of me and loving me.

I believe that Teddy was sent to teach and heal me. Teddy is still with me, whispering reminders when I get off track.

I am listening, my beloved Teddy.

Meditation

Has a cat ever taken on a condition or karma for you? What did you learn from a cat whose experience mirrored yours?

The Music of Forever Love

Beverly F. Walker
Greenbrier, Tennessee

*M*y son Donnie died so suddenly. They told us that he fell asleep at the wheel. The blessed shock and numbness I felt keeps me from remembering everything about the drive from Tennessee to his apartment in North Carolina. I'll never forget walking into his room, where he had slept, and falling onto his bed, wailing like someone had torn out my very heart. My husband, my oldest son, and my daughter closed the bedroom door and left me there for a time. I could barely breathe.

This was after the visit to the hospital where my son's body had been taken. He lay in an autopsy room beneath the floor where we sat in a small room. The hospital chaplain consoled us, when all I wanted were Donnie's belongings — something of his that I could hold on to. I cannot describe everything I was going through: the disbelief that he was gone, the frustration, the anger, and the overwhelming sadness. If you are a mother, or if you are merely a human being on this planet, you can imagine how horrid and grief-filled this day was for my family and me. I only wanted to be with my son, and I had no earthly idea how I could go on living without him.

Putting one foot in front of the other, we left the hospital and drove to Donnie's apartment. I remember looking at Donnie's things and thinking, "This is all that is left of my son." The handful of possessions in his small apartment spoke of a struggling young man trying to make it in the world of music. His master of music degree was framed and hanging on a wall. Seeing it there caused my soul to swell with pride. But my tears started again as I contemplated the fatal conclusion to Donnie's plans for the future. After gathering a few of my son's precious belongings, including his classical guitar, we headed back to Tennessee to face the funeral, the burial, and a gathering of loved ones and friends. My oldest son drove his truck back to North Carolina the following week to retrieve the remainder of Donnie's things.

One of the "things" that needed a new home was Donny's cat, Audrey. Donnie had gotten Audrey from an animal shelter approximately three years earlier, and had named her after Audrey Hepburn, his favorite actress. Since my husband and I already had a cat, Donnie's stepsister Charlene took Audrey to live with her in North Carolina.

Audrey lived with Charlene and her family for nearly four years after my son died. Then, after we moved to a new house, our cat ran away. As hard as we tried, we never could find him. When Charlene said that she, too, was planning to move to a new home, I inquired about Audrey. "Would you be willing to let us have Audrey now?" I asked.

I didn't really think Charlene would part with her brother's cat, but to my surprise, she said, "Sure." I think she must have known that we, too, needed the comfort of this cat who had been such a good friend to Donnie.

We made arrangements to get Audrey. On a lovely spring day, we drove to Charlene's home to pick up Donnie's cat. "You'll feel connected to Donnie around her," Charlene said as we put Audrey in the cat carrier. "I always feel Donnie when Audrey is in the room." We hugged and said our good-byes, and Donnie's cat was on her way to a new home.

After we returned home, Audrey spent most of the time hiding. She wasn't sure about this new place. A skittish sort of cat, Audrey did not like noises or other pets, yet she had to get used to our dog, Shiloh. We decided to just let her hide and adjust according to her own schedule. I began to grow impatient, though, wanting to give her love and have her get to know me.

Beverly's Audrey

For about a month, Audrey came out only to eat and to run from one hiding place to another. However, one spring day when I was really missing Donnie, I put on a recording of his guitar recital. He'd made the tape during his junior year at Vanderbilt's Blair School of Music. Soon after the music began, I saw Audrey peek out from under the bed. She tentatively emerged, meowed a few times, and seemed to look around, as if on a search mission. In seconds, she was purring and gliding along my legs. She remembered Donnie; I'm sure of it! Her love for my son had drawn her out, and she connected to him in a truly spiritual way.

I immediately went to get Donnie's quilt, which was on his bed, and laid it out on the floor. Then I picked Audrey up and placed her on top of the quilt. I had not washed it since Donnie's death, and I remembered how Audrey often had slept on it at his apartment. Now she began to purr even more, rolling over and rubbing herself on the quilt.

Since that day when the cat and I bonded over my son's music and quilt, Audrey seems to realize that there is love for her in our home. I think she knows that we are connected to the wonderful young man who first adopted her. Being my son's cat, she could not help but cultivate a love for his music. Art and music were this "Renaissance man's" first love, and he played many varieties of music in his apartment nearly every day. Audrey must have spent hours listening to him play his own music as well.

Audrey still doesn't let us pet her unless she's in the mood for it. I call her my "prissy missy with an attitude." But it only takes a little music to soothe her and bring her near — especially classical music, and always the music my son used to play on his guitar. She is truly an angel pet, connecting me spiritually with Donnie forever.

Meditation

Have you and a cat ever grieved together over the loss of a loved one? Did you miss signs of the cat's grief? How has a cat comforted you in your times of sorrow?

Tough Guy

Pamela Jenkins
Henryetta, Oklahoma

When I saw the tangled mass of hair and the cat's listless expression, I knew I had to do something. I'd been noticing this black cat around our barn for about two weeks. Always shy, he would slink away whenever he saw me doing chores. On this morning, however, he paused and looked back over his shoulder. In that brief instant, as we stared at each other, I felt his mixture of distrust and hope.

I went to the tack room of the barn and pulled out the Havahart trap, which safely secures animals. That night, I left it by the barn door with an open can of sardines inside.

The next morning, I found the trap door closed. Inside the trap sat the cat, and I was finally able to get a better look at him. He seemed to be a Persian cat with big eyes and a flat nose. Unfortunately, his lower jaw stuck out far enough that his bottom teeth showed. He had a funny, bulldoglike face. It reminded me of a tough guy in an old gangster movie. Since the cat seemed to be having a hard time surviving on his own, my husband and I decided to give him a "tough guy" name. We called him Bullet.

That morning, Bullet rode with me to the veterinary clinic where I work. He didn't seem at all frightened by the movement of the car. In fact, he didn't seem to care one way or the other what we did with him. It was as if all the struggling he had endured had taken the life out of him.

Pamela's Bullet

Over the next few days, Bullet got a complete makeover at the clinic. He tested negative for feline diseases, received his vaccinations, and was neutered. I put him on a healthy diet. We cleaned the mites out of his ears and medicated the many wounds he'd accumulated through catfights. The biggest change for the scruffy Bullet was when we relieved him of years' worth of neglected hair coat. We had to completely shave him. All that was left were his whiskers and a tuft on the end of his tail. Even with his new hairdo, Bullet looked rough. His body was covered with scars from parasites and injuries, and his ears were notched from battles with other cats.

Bullet accepted all our ministrations with patience and grace. He obviously had been someone's pet at one time; no feral cat would have tolerated the grooming we put him through. But in spite of all the attention we lavished on him, Bullet remained aloof and shy. In an attempt to help him feel more at ease at the clinic, I gave him a cardboard box. Lined with a soft baby blanket, it was just what he wanted: a safe, comfortable den away from the world, which had been so unkind to him.

When Bullet at last came home with me from the vet's office, he would step out of his cardboard box only long enough to eat or drink. Then he'd hurry back to his sanctuary. My other cats seemed to understand that the box had to be Bullet's space, and they let him be alone in it. He was content to spend his time in solitude.

Several weeks went by with little change in Bullet's behavior. He continued to heal, and his hair grew back with a lustrous shine. His frame filled out as he settled into our home. Still, our new cat remained quiet and stayed out of sight.

One day, I was sitting in my rocking chair in front of the French doors. I had just been through a stressful week, and I was feeling low. At times, depression overwhelms me. This is a battle I face every day. My family was gone at the moment, and I found myself alone with my sad thoughts. As I watched the busy birds outside at the feeder, I wiped a tear from my cheek.

Then I saw movement off to my side. Bullet stood in the living room. He was looking back to where a tuft of fur waved slowly back and forth at the end of his tail. He suddenly spun around and swatted it, chasing his tail in a circle as if he had found his own personal toy. I held my breath, watching this cat actually play for the first time. After a while, he lost interest. He slowly walked over to me and sat down at my feet, looking up into my eyes.

"Hey, Bullet," I said softly. "You've come out to play today, huh?"

In the next instant, for the first time, Bullet launched himself onto my lap and curled up in a ball. Also for the first time, I heard his deep, rumbling purr of contentment. "This is just what I need today," I thought as I stroked his coat. Then Bullet swiveled his bulldog face so that he could gaze at me. Slowly, he winked his eyes.

I will never know what happened in Bullet's life before he came into mine. Whatever his traumatic history may have been, on that day I could see that he was slowly overcoming his fears and reservations. He was beginning to forget his past hurts and live again. He had overcome being abandoned and unloved — one of the biggest obstacles anyone ever has to face. As I rubbed the spot behind his ears, Bullet's purring grew even louder. In an instant, listening to this cat's gentle purr, my own problems didn't seem so insurmountable after all.

Since that afternoon, Bullet has snuggled up beside me many times when I've been feeling down. Somehow he knows when his presence will help me the most. He may have needed a helping hand on that day long ago when I found him in the barn, but this old tough guy has paid me back a thousand times over with his love.

Meditation

How have cats shown you ways to overcome feelings of abandonment? Is there a cat in your life who serves as Divine relief from depression?

A Morning Home Alone

Tim Bellows
Gold River, California

My wife's cat, Sir Riley,
shadowed past me as I stood
in the linty, fluorescent laundry room,

half lost, half
found inside my tiny notebook,
a loamy, procreating field where I

make up skies and a blue lake
sliced by translucent wind.
Now a marvel of cat shadow

skittered, beckoning me as I entertained a wish
for a gliding, magic life. He roughhoused with himself —
lightly, down the long beige rectangle, our back hall.

His shoulder blades gyrated with spells,
with composure worth twice the price
of any dusky Mona Lisa. If I would only

wake up and follow him,
golden eyes and a million small suns
would hum and shine along the ceilings

of this empty house.

Tim's Sir Riley

Meditation

What would happen if you followed a cat's lead? What artistic, creative, and spiritual pathways would you find glowing with a golden light?

A Life Lesson from Two Cats

Bettine Clemen
Seymour, Missouri

A few days after my husband, Peter, and I moved into our new timber-frame home in the Ozarks, we were adopted first by a huge white Great Pyrenees dog and shortly afterward by a beautiful calico cat. Every evening at around six o'clock, this pretty cat showed up on our deck, waiting to be fed. She ate, stayed just a bit, and then disappeared. She was shy at first, but we always enjoyed her company even though it was so temporary. Gradually, she became more friendly and trusting; at times, she even ventured into the house. By the time winter came, our walk-in calico lady had established herself in our home as our beloved Alpha, the name we affectionately began to call her.

Soon Alpha ruled our house. She slept most of the day, lounging on sofas and chairs and practicing the very high art form of conserving energy, at which cats are masters. After a relaxing day, she would have her evening meal. If we did not deliver her food precisely on time, she would demand it by making sweet, babylike noises that left no doubt that she wanted her well-deserved meal for working so hard all day.

After dinner, Alpha would turn into a wild tiger and disappear into our garden. I watched her secretly a few times. She had tremendous adventures, such as suddenly attacking a bush, or jumping onto a fence, or focusing on a hole in our stable wall with that amazing presence and focus cats have. Every morning at precisely seven, as punctual as a German clock, Alpha would sit in front of our glass patio doors, waiting to be let in for her morning treat: some dry cat food. Then she would jump onto our bed and begin her day by falling asleep once again.

Alpha had definitely become an important part of our ever-growing menagerie. By the time she started sharing our home, our animal family included two horses named Angelo and Amadeus; a donkey named Dominique; Harry Trotter, a potbellied pig who had wandered onto our property from the surrounding forests; and our dog, Orbit. For some time, we all lived together in wonderful harmony until one day a visitor disturbed our peaceful existence.

On a spring evening, a neighbor's huge gray tomcat arrived on our patio deck. Alpha's food bowl was there. Immediately Mac, short for Machiavelli, hissed at Alpha and then attacked her food. He brazenly ate it all in front of her. I was stunned. Alpha became submissive, hid in a corner, and let Mac steal her food. When Mac disappeared after having his fill, I felt relieved. I hoped that he'd come for a one-time visit and wouldn't bother us again. But the next evening, there he was again.

This time, Alpha immediately disappeared as soon as she saw Mac. Again, he ate her food. I felt angry, not only at Mac, but also at Alpha. How could she be so passive and let him do this to her? I wanted Alpha to be more assertive and not give in to a "macho man," even if he looked strong and menacing.

The ocean behind the wave of emotion I felt had more to do

with me than with Alpha, though. I recognized that this cat was behaving as I had in the past. So often in my life, I had allowed strong, authoritarian men to run over my wants and desires. I had much too frequently given in to their plans instead of standing up for myself. The more I related to Alpha's predicament with Mac, the more my anger grew. For the second time, I watched Mac eat placidly while Alpha sat in a faraway corner, pouting and looking afraid. Before I even knew what I was saying, I shouted at Mac, "Get lost, you idiot! I never want to see you here again! Eat your own food! Leave us alone!"

My rage must have startled the cat, for I was surprised to see Mac shiver and run off into the dark. I picked up Alpha and cradled her in my arms. Then I refilled her food bowl. "Alpha," I scolded, "you have to learn to stand up for yourself!"

The next day around noon, our neighbor called. "I don't know what to do," she said. "Mac has suddenly become very ill. He can hardly move. He is lying in a corner and doesn't eat or drink. The vet thinks he ate some rat poison or something like that. Can you come over?"

My heart sank at the news: Mac was deathly ill. And I had yelled at him the night before, expressing anger more strongly than I had ever intended. I wondered if Mac had become sick because I had directed the poison of my anger at him. Guilt settled into my heart. What if I were the reason for his sudden illness?

My mind raced back to more disturbing memories. Several years before, my mother had died soon after I had hung up on her following an angry exchange of words. Having her die without being able to make up with her has been one of the toughest experiences in my life. So here I was in a similar situation, with Mac now dying. Would his last memory of me be my angry voice? Or would we have the chance to heal — an opportunity that had been denied me with my mother?

I immediately drove over to see Mac. He looked dreadful. The life force had almost gone out of him, and he didn't move. I ran back to our house and got some herbal medicine that had done miracles for people and animals alike. With a dropper, my friend and I inserted the liquid into Mac's mouth. After about ten doses, Mac started to move a bit. He looked at us with big, sad eyes. "Look, he's getting better!" I shouted hopefully. "Mac, come on, you can make it!"

We continued our therapy. I even took out the Tibetan flute I had brought along and played some soft music for him. He seemed to rally. We gave him more herbs, more love, more petting. I repeatedly told Mac that I was sorry I'd yelled at him and chased him away in anger. He was struggling to survive, though, and I wasn't certain he understood or accepted my apologies.

My neighbor and I thought that Mac must be getting better, but then without warning he took a turn for the worse. His legs started to stiffen, and he grew cold. After what seemed like an eternity of suffering, which really lasted only a few minutes, Mac died.

My neighbor and I were devastated. I went home and cried desperately. For the second time in my life, I had hurt a fellow creature who then died shortly after my angry outburst. Even though I'd been able to apologize to Mac, how could I forgive myself for having gotten so upset with him? And had Mac actually forgiven me?

Several days later, our neighbors and I buried Mac. Each of us took a moment to say good-bye to him. When my turn came, I cried uncontrollably: "Mac, please forgive me," I pleaded. "I didn't want to hurt you. I was just upset because of Alpha. I never meant to cause you pain!" That night, I went home and mourned for a cat named Mac.

When I returned from Mac's burial, Alpha was in the house. She immediately jumped up onto my lap to comfort me, soothing my anguish with her gentle presence. My words to the cat spoke of the pain and remorse I felt not only for Mac, but also for my mother. "Alpha," I said as she looked at me with her penetrating golden eyes, "both you and Mac have taught me a deep spiritual lesson: I will never, ever direct anger at any creature, person, or animal — not even at a plant! Such anger is destructive energy. It can injure!

Bettine's Alpha

And you, Alpha, taught me to let others always choose their own actions and responses. It was none of my business to tell you how to deal with Mac."

Alpha gazed at me with deep love and understanding. I knew then that she would help me heal, and she did.

During the weeks after Mac's death, Alpha let me know that I had not failed and that I was not being judged by anyone but myself. She comforted me by simply being nearby whenever I felt sad. She would jump onto my lap and look at me with great compassion. When I did my yoga exercises, she started lying on top of me during the closing relaxation movements, her breathing perfectly coordinated with mine. It was as if she knew that I needed her to be an integral part of my recovery. Eventually, I was also able to transfer the ability to forgive myself for hurting Mac to the dreadful situation that had occurred with my mother's death. I understood that my mother, like Mac, had not carried the sting of my anger beyond her existence in this world. I realized that our love for each other would never die.

Later, I also concluded that Alpha and Mac had mirrored for me what I had gone through so often with dominant males. These two cats, with the scene they played out before my eyes, showed me that I must be true to myself regardless of what an assertive man might want me to do. I don't have to give away my power or be submissive because of someone I perceive to be stronger than me. I took to heart the lesson Alpha and Mac taught. Now I try my best to be the source for my life without living it in reaction to others.

Every day, Alpha continues to accept and love me totally. She lights up my life with her sweet presence and teaches me to treasure her gift of unconditional love.

Meditation

Are you able to look back on an experience with a cat that clearly reflects your own spiritual lessons in life? What has the Divine been able to show you about yourself and your life through a cat's eyes?

Hocus and a World of Ordinary Miracles

Sally Rosenthal
Philadelphia, Pennsylvania

As the aroma of brewing coffee permeates my early-morning kitchen, I settle down at the table and wait for the perking to stop. Just as it does every morning, a small black-and-white paw gently taps my leg, announcing Hocus's arrival on the chair beside me. I reach over to stroke her head, and she steps onto my lap before leaping gingerly onto the table for her customary greeting.

Although her movements might have slowed a bit over the fourteen years she has lived with me, Hocus never misses an opportunity to share a moment of affection and friendship. Her formerly rotund body, stretched out luxuriously on the table, feels a little thinner and more frail beneath my hand, but, I reason, neither of us is as young as we once were. My old friend, purring now at my touch, and I have both weathered storms during our time together. We have weathered them, yes, but we came through with some of the wrinkles and wisdom associated with age.

While waiting for the coffee this morning, I touch noses with Hocus and think again about the comfort she brings me every day and what a blessing she has become over the years. I never realized, when my husband and I adopted Hocus and her late sister, Pocus, as feral kittens, just how much this rather plain, easily overlooked tuxedo cat would mean to me.

Hocus was not our only cat, nor was she the most memorable at first impression. Her feisty littermate, Pocus, reserved her affections for my husband and me, choosing to meet strangers with an attitude worthy of her feral heritage. Neither we who loved her nor those who saw only her more skittish side could forget Pocus.

Ziggy, our sweet-natured tabby, greeted the world with joy before he finally succumbed to cardiomyopathy. He lived with an open heart, and he fully expected the world to meet him on equal terms. He was not disappointed; no one who met Ziggy could resist his charms or fail to fall in love with him.

Shadow, our rescued diabetic stray ginger tabby, warmed to human contact and impressed all who met him with his humble and

Sally's Hocus

trusting personality. And Toby, our youngest former stray, was such an outgoing sprite that she amused everyone who came under her spell.

Hocus entered our lives when my husband, Sandy, and I began dating in middle age. After our marriage, Sandy's post-polio syndrome worsened, causing him to make many difficult changes. Although he had been able to walk with crutches and braces when we first met, increasing fatigue and pain caused Sandy to move to a manual wheelchair and eventually to a power wheelchair. He had to trade in his car for a ramped converted van. At the same time, my vision slowly slipped away as a result of delayed-onset retinopathy of prematurity and glaucoma. I had to leave behind consecutive careers as a college librarian and an occupational therapist, and I became increasingly isolated at home.

Over the years that I shared my home with Hocus, my father died; my mother aged, with many of the problems that accompany the process; and my only brother survived a heart attack. Time took a toll on our feline family, too, as Pocus and Ziggy passed away.

Usually resilient, I often felt worn out and overwhelmed by all the changes. Life could, at times, seem out of my control. It was hard not to feel left behind in a world that had become smaller on a daily basis. Once I had been able to drive and use public transportation; now I found myself unable to travel farther than my mailbox, even while using my white cane. Many friends and former colleagues seemed uncomfortable around me and at a loss for how to help. Fewer and fewer people returned my phone calls. Good friends remained, but their number became smaller and many did not live nearby, so I grew increasingly isolated. I had always been active and productive. Now I wondered how I could still contribute in a meaningful way.

As I wondered about the direction my life was taking, Hocus would sleep on my lap, nuzzle my hand in comfort, and give me strength through her very presence. The small acts of kindness that she, who had begun life as a fearful feral, performed so unselfishly caused me to consider how valuable such seemingly unobtrusive acts can be.

Through all my challenging experiences, quiet, unassuming Hocus would not have stood out to the casual observer as a hero. She was, as I often consoled her, steadfast in a world that did not always honor such qualities. Over the years, Hocus's presence during the events in our lives caused me to realize just what precious qualities steadfastness and friendship truly are.

Hocus has caused me to view small acts with greater respect. Whether I am giving or receiving an act of comfort or kindness, donating time or money to a worthy cause, or writing a book review through which I share another animal's story, each small act connects me with the world in a circle of compassion. As Hocus has taught me, the "small" is never really small.

I prefer to call these little acts "ordinary miracles." They occur each day, but they're often overlooked in the light of bigger acts or events. The small things in life have much in common, I muse, with the cat who shares my early-morning coffee every day. In her quiet, gentle way, Hocus is the embodiment of ordinary miracles. I make it a practice to never overlook her or them.

Meditation

How do cats help you realize that "small acts" and "ordinary miracles" are treasures of immeasurable worth?

Ask Cuddles

Dear Cuddles,

When cats look in the mirror, what do they see?

Sincerely,
Curious

Dear Curious,

When we cats look in the mirror, we see a Divine
spark of God clothed in a furry body. Of course, we
see Divine sparks of God when we look into the eyes
of our human friends as well -- even the ones who
don't know that this is what they truly are.

Transcendentally yours,
Cuddles

So far, all of the stories in this book have demonstrated the spiritual nature of cats and how they illuminate the golden threads that connect all of life. In the next chapter, these connections will shine even more brightly as we meet cats on earth and in heaven who more than live up to their mystical, supernatural heritage.

CHAPTER FIVE

Will We Hear the Sound of a Heavenly Purr?

Tybalt: What wouldst thou have with me?
Mercutio: Good King of Cats, nothing but one of your nine lives.

— William Shakespeare, *Romeo and Juliet*, Act III, 1:77

*F*ree will is a spiritual quality that humans tend to think only they possess. Yet cats and other animals consistently demonstrate the fact that they have the wisdom and determination to make choices. For example, our cat Speedy loves the cable television station Animal Planet. He waits patiently in front of a blank screen for us to notice that he's missing his favorite shows. With those brilliant green eyes pleading for a favor, we can't resist turning on the television and joining this little couch potato for a purring good time. His fascination becomes contagious. Oh, how difficult it is to get any work done in a house that is ruled by the cat we have nicknamed our Lion King!

Awareness, creativity, preferences, discrimination (or free will), unconditional love, and altruism are qualities that most of us who live with cats have seen displayed in abundance. These are spiritual traits that humans wish they had more of. Spirituality and cats seem to be entwined throughout history. It is said that the myth of the nine lives cats are supposed to have originates from, among other legends, "the number of times that Muhammad stroked his cat Muezza when the cat thanked the prophet for his graciousness. Muhammad had cut off his sleeve rather than disturb Muezza, who had been sleeping on the soft fabric."[1]

Even with all the references to cats in sacred literature, some people have a hard time believing that an animal's soul lives on after death. It's understandable that we should wonder about these mysteries of life and death. Many people are uncertain, although hopeful, that there is an afterlife for themselves, much less for their beloved pets. Others possessively guard the pearly gates and quote selected passages from scriptures and theological scholars to prove that God will not, under any circumstances, allow animals into heaven. It is as if they have forgotten that God is...well, God. If God wants animals to be with us in heaven, then the Divine is perfectly capable of saying, as Captain Picard commands on *Star Trek,* "Make it so."

This chapter presents stories that reveal incredible aspects of the cat kingdom's uniquely spiritual nature. You are about to meet cats who have the ability to heal, to pray, to protect, and to leave signs that, after death, only their physical bodies have left this earthly plane. We hope the following stories and spiritual experiences will bring comfort to all who grieve the loss of beloved cat companions.

The Man Who Got His Purr Back

Tim Miejan
Woodbury, Minnesota

*C*hina Cat Sunflower, one of the most intelligent animals I have ever known, and Lady Madonna were with me for seventeen years and fifteen years, respectively, sharing my home in Missouri and then Minnesota. I bought them in 1986 for twenty-five dollars each from a woman who lived in a trailer in rural Missouri. These two cats spent years running the length of my bungalow-style apartment at breakneck speed, and they seemed to be in good condition for middle-aged cats. Rounding out the trio of my closest friends in life was my cat Seth, a domestic shorthair with a dark body and wild-looking stripes, who possesses an almost Zen-like calm. He's been with me for about ten of his fourteen years. I rescued him from a farm he shared with scores of other cats, three dogs, one horse, and a donkey.

Since these three cats were with me through my life's highs and lows, I wanted to better understand their behavior. I especially appreciated how they always tried to keep me from stressing out by questioning me sternly — and quite vocally — whenever I raised my voice in upset. One occasion stands out in my memory, though I didn't fully understand at the time how my cats were helping me. Months before I moved to Minnesota in 1995, I suffered an appendicitis-like pain that was later diagnosed as a spastic colon. As I lay on the floor of my apartment, waiting for my mother to arrive to take me to the hospital, China sat at my head, Madonna flanked my right leg, and Seth stayed by my left leg. It seemed to me that the cats were triangulating me in a group healing session.

About five months later, we moved to Minnesota. At that time, I invited Teri Ann, a "pet whisperer" from the AnimalSpeak Company, to come talk with my three cats so that I could learn more about them. Teri communicates with pets through visual images, something she says all of us can do if we understand how animals talk. I'll never forget the experience of watching my cats interact with her that day. It left a mark on my relationship with them, particularly with my two apple-headed Siamese, China and Madonna. I asked Teri to question Madonna about that healing experience in Missouri. I was surprised by her response.

"They were not in a triangle on purpose," Teri said, "but they were around you because you had lost your purr. They hear your vibration — your *chi*, your life force — as if it were purring. On that day, you lost your purr, and they were worried that you weren't coming back. They were around you, purring, to help recharge you."

Those words seemed so perfect in that moment. Remembering that day when I was sick, I realized that what she said was true: I had lost my purr. That sudden bout of pain had been brought on by increasing stress in my being. At the time, I felt as if I had been treading water in my life. My job with the same employer for thirteen years seemed to be going nowhere. The workload was increasing exponentially as the pages of the calendar flipped by. I badly needed change. Without knowing it at the time, I was having a meltdown. Some people suffer panic attacks; I suffered a revolt in my intestines. I had, indeed, lost my purr.

Upon hearing Teri's comments, I realized that, although I had not read the signals, my three roommates had been more in tune with my situation than I had been. I also recalled that, in recent years, when I lay down to sleep, the three cats would snuggle near my head, my side, and my feet. I wondered if they were monitoring my condition, recharging my purr.

I often moved them in order to sleep more comfortably, but Teri said they surrounded me so that they could do their work. I told her that, because I moved around so often during the day, the cats had few opportunities to be near me. "Take more naps," she advised, "so that the cats have another chance to be close to you."

Tim's Seth

Madonna, the heavier of the two Siamese sisters, told Teri that she chases uninvited energy away from me while I work at my computer. Considering herself a queen (interestingly, my wife had nicknamed her Miss Regal), Madonna's job was to protect me. She often delegated that job to Seth, who sometimes felt bossed around by Madonna.

I mentioned to Teri a puzzling habit of Madonna's: She would meow insistently whenever I hung up the phone. Teri relayed to me that Madonna was concerned about me because she thought I was speaking to air. She didn't understand what I was doing, and, frankly, she thought I was losing my mind. So she was telling me that she was there for me if I wanted to speak to somebody. Teri took the opportunity to explain to Madonna in general terms that I am talking to another person when I hold the phone, but Madonna communicated to Teri that she would prefer for me to speak exclusively to her. I smiled, because I knew that this cat had always been very devoted to me.

Seth had grown up on a small farm in the home of a coworker whom I used to visit often. Seth told Teri that he used to sleep in a cold barn and that he was very thankful that I'd rescued him. He said that he loves the soft blankets and warm home he now enjoys with me.

Teri learned something else that surprised me at the time: China confided that she was a warrior in a cat's body. Speaking with a single-pointed glare, as if she were sending laser beams of information directly into the pet whisperer's brain, China showed Teri the origin of her soul. China's eyes turned to snakelike slits as she "talked" about her history. Her true name, she told Teri, was unpronounce-able. She disliked the name China, considering it too dainty, so I decided to start saying her name with more vigor, in a more warrior-like way: "Chi-NAH!"

Tim's Madonna (top) and China (bottom)

The cats all took turns speaking with Teri, looking at her calmly and making direct eye contact. They didn't make a single sound the entire time Teri was with us. After she left, I gathered my companions around me and sent love to them, and I felt it returned.

As I reflected on this session with the pet whisperer, I realized how accurate the cats had been when they triangulated me in a group healing session on the floor of my Missouri apartment. They had astutely noticed that my spirit was draining and my body was in trouble.

Following a three-day hospital stay, I had come home and made drastic changes in my life. I moved to Minnesota, married for the first time, and settled into a new role as father to my wife's young son. I found a rewarding job that was less stressful, and I was able to work at home and spend more time with my pets. The excruciating pain in my body has never returned. In some respects, I thank my four-legged friends for helping me stay relaxed, more attuned with my body, and in harmony with my purr.

Madonna left her body near Christmas in 2001. Her sister China lowered her head in my hands for the final time in May of 2003. Seth is still with me, but he's getting noticeably older and losing weight.

As a result of my experiences with China, Madonna, and Seth, I came to more fully feel the interconnectedness between animals and humans. Strip away the external bodies, and you have beings of energy interacting with other beings of energy. If only everyone knew that, the world would be a more loving place.

Meditation

Have you lost your purr? Are you allowing the cat or cats in your life to help restore your life force through their special connection with you and the Divine?

Tigger Purrs a Love Song to God

Carole Punt
Kaleden, British Columbia

*A*s I walked to work early one spring morning, a gray tabby kitten jumped down from his perch on a porch railing and ran over to me. I stooped to greet him. When I continued on my way, the little one followed me. Each time I picked him up and returned him to his porch, he leaped down and followed me again. I finally gave up, thinking he would soon become weary of this venture and return home. To my amazement, though, he trotted after me like a dog trained to heel. I had never seen a cat do that before!

I knew the kitten wasn't a stray because he wore a collar and had a healthy coat. After walking several blocks, I picked him up and carried him back to his home. This time, I noticed that the front door of his house was slightly ajar, so I set him inside and shut the door.

I am a person who watches for waking dreams in my life. Waking dreams are usually experiences or images that catch our attention, sometimes dramatically. They are messages from Spirit that offer direction or guidance — often in answer to a request or a question. As with any dream symbolism, a waking dream must be noticed, remembered, and interpreted by its recipient.

Having been so persistently followed by the kitten that day, I began to wonder if he was a waking dream sent to deliver a message from Spirit. Could it be that my husband, Phil, and I should consider bringing a pet into our lives? After forty-five years of marriage, our children were grown and it was just the two of us in our house. For several years, we had enjoyed our two small "granddogs" — our children's dogs, Charlie and Chess — but we hadn't had a pet of our own for about twenty years, nor had we been considering the idea. I've learned, however, that Spirit knows what we need better than we do. I wondered if Spirit knew that my husband and I would benefit from the renewed emphasis on giving and receiving love that sharing one's life with a pet brings into a person's life.

A few days after the gray tabby befriended me, I sat in a lawn chair at home, reading and relaxing in the sun. Soon a neighbor's black cat, Stella, jumped into my lap and made herself comfortable. Stella is a rather large cat with a loving but somewhat shy nature. "Hmmm, this is odd," I thought. Stella had come to visit on previous occasions when I had sat on the lawn of our small apartment building enjoying the sun. Her visits had always been brief, as she stopped to let me pet and talk to her. This was the first time she'd jumped onto my lap.

After these two cat visitors, I decided to make a formal request to Spirit: "If we're supposed to bring a kitten into our home, please give me one more sign by Sunday night."

The next Sunday morning, as I was preparing for the day, a large gray tabby cat sauntered into our bathroom. I was astonished! It was a warm morning, and I had left our apartment door ajar to allow the morning breeze to enter. I didn't know the name of this large tabby, but I recognized her as having recently moved into a house across the back lane. The cat had caught my eye as I'd seen her riding on her human companion's shoulder when the woman bicycled down the lane.

I considered myself a dog person, and so did my husband. Cats had not been part of our life since our son and daughter were in high school. Now, within days, I'd had three cats dropped in my lap, so to speak. I couldn't ignore the message. In response to my request for one more waking dream by Sunday night, Spirit hadn't wasted any time.

Now I knew that I had to share my waking-dream experiences with Phil. I explained that I felt Spirit was asking us to bring a kitten into our lives. At first, my husband resisted the idea. He was concerned about the inconvenience, work, and responsibility of having our own pet. A few days earlier, I'd been attracted to a notice on a store bulletin board offering free kittens. The next day, after talking with Phil, I couldn't resist returning to the store to get the phone number for the kittens who needed a home. After considerable coaxing from me and other family members, Phil agreed to take a look at the kittens. He understands messages from Spirit, too, so it was hard for him to ignore my waking dreams.

At last, we drove across town to visit the new kittens. When I picked up one of them, he leaped from my arms and ran away. The second kitten I cradled in my arms cuddled up and settled in as if he were meant to be there. Within minutes, Phil and I drove off with our new pet.

The kitten meowed loudly as we drove back into town and then carried him into the pet store for necessary supplies, but he quieted down as soon as I released him in our apartment. By that time, my reluctant husband had fallen in love with our new furry friend. Phil suggested that we call the cat Tigger, as the name had spontaneously popped into his mind. Tigger soon calmed down and felt safe again. From that day on, he engaged us in games as we played hide-and-seek or pulled him around in a shoebox.

In the mornings, Tigger would cuddle up beside Phil as Phil did his daily spiritual exercise. Spiritual exercise is a time when we each spend about twenty minutes in contemplation to help us gain inner direction from Spirit. We start our spiritual exercises by singing "HU" (which rhymes with the word *blue),* a sacred name for God. HU is an ancient love song that is sung like a chant or mantra on a long, exhaled breath while you fill your heart with love. A few mornings after Tigger came home

Carole's Tigger

with us, Phil said that he'd heard the kitten singing HU with him. The cat was making a sound Phil hadn't heard from him before: "It is a mew that sounds like HU," he said.

Several weeks later, Phil, Tigger, and I moved to a new home in another town. On the first day after settling in, my husband and I sat together to do our morning spiritual exercise, with Tigger lying beside us. That's when I also heard the HU in Tigger's mew!

I believe that we, as humans, are soul. We use our physical bodies to experience life and learn our lessons about love. I believe that animals are soul, too. As soul, we are each Divine sparks of God. Singing HU connects us with the love in all of life that is flowing from the heart of God. As soul, animals find ways to express their love for God, too. We were blessed to hear Tigger express his love with the sound of HU in his mew.

Meditation

Would you like to try singing HU with a cat? Get comfortable with your little critter at a time and in a place where you won't be disturbed for a while. Take a deep breath. On any note, sing a long, drawn-out HU-U-U-U with the exhaled breath. Relax. Repeat for about five or ten minutes. Give yourself another five or ten minutes of silence to reflect on the spiritual connection you have with this cat, or on any other aspect of your relationship. How does this cat help you love God more?

Bears Are No Match for KittyBaby

Nancy Strand
Petersburg, Alaska

*K*ittyBaby arrived in our wooded yard after apparently being abandoned by his previous family. We live in Petersburg, in the middle of the Tongass National Forest of southeastern Alaska, a temperate rainforest. Rainfall is measured in feet here, and the summer when KittyBaby arrived was a fairly average rainy season. At that time, our designer cat, Feral, a beautiful chinchilla Persian, lived with us. As an adolescent, Feral had also been abandoned in a nearby park, and had arrived on our doorstep on the Ides of March. Soon, Feral had taken over our little cabin in the woods and was happy to command the entire house, yard, and beach.

Our house has one smallish room, and it sits on a tiny cove that contains a local city park and a few much larger homes. We are nestled on a wooded third-of-an-acre lot and enjoy the feeling of pristine solitude, while also being privileged to have convenient access to town and amenities. Our front yard is the beach, and the backyard has abundant foliage. The landscaping is natural, cool, and quiet.

When KittyBaby showed up at our cabin, he was ragged-looking and had a torn ear that he'd obviously acquired in a dangerous incident or a fight. A hulking sort of cat, he had broad shoulders and a

Nancy's KittyBaby

striding gait. He reminded me of a big biker cat, yet he was a gentle love. At first, Feral was wary of KittyBaby and kept him at bay. I finally told Feral that we really should let KittyBaby stay since he was homeless, cold, and hungry — the way *she* had been when she arrived on our doorstep. So Kitty-Baby joined our little household in the woods, and we enjoyed a tenuous peace.

Meanwhile, a mile or so away from us, a change was taking place that would affect and even threaten us. The local municipality had started baling at the garbage dump. This meant that the garbage was bound into huge bales and shipped outside Alaska to other states, where it would be recycled or composted. The year before the baling began, the Fish and Game Department had transported over thirty black bears to outlying islands. The great bear transfer had involved tranquilizing thirty-three bears and flying them, slung below a helicopter, out to Kulu Island, as well as transporting two cinnamon bears to the mainland. Many of the bears had made their way back to our area in anticipation of this summer's trash picking, which was no longer an option due to the baling. Suddenly the bears, who had been eating a free lunch at the dump for many generations, didn't have access to food in the garbage that humans usually threw away.

Now the bears had to get their dinner from other sources. Naturally, they looked for the path of least resistance. Until the local streams filled with salmon and the berries ripened, the bears turned to scrounging food from residential garbage cans. Because we separated our trash and recycled it, we put out only one small bag of garbage each week. On pickup day, I always placed the bag in our garbage can by the road, near where our car was parked about two hundred feet from the cabin.

After bears started passing through our neighborhood, Kitty-Baby quickly made himself invaluable. One night, as I prepared to go outside, KittyBaby firmly pushed me away from the door. He pressed hard against my leg, redirecting me to another area. The next morning, I discovered that a marauding bear had turned over and ransacked our garbage can during the night. This was the first time I realized that KittyBaby was protecting us from bears. On numerous other occasions when KittyBaby sensed a bear nearby, he would stand between me and the cat flap on the door and growl as if he were a big dog!

During the season when the bears were scavenging for food in our neighborhood, I had a little janitorial job that required me to leave the house at two or three o'clock in the morning. Each morning when I returned from work, KittyBaby would meet me up at the road to let me know there were no bears around. If he wasn't on the road when I got home, I waited in the car until he came up to escort me down the path. KittyBaby's absence was my sign that there was probably a little blackie in the area; showing up was his signal that the coast was clear. Neither of us was brave or foolish enough to venture out if there was a bruin in the neighborhood.

A couple of years ago, my KittyBaby died suddenly in my arms. We had no warning of any illness, and the vet told me that the cat had probably had a heart attack or a stroke. We were bereft when our big guy left us so suddenly. But we are waiting for him to return someday. Maybe he's already here, and we just haven't noticed yet. I sometimes think that KittyBaby must still be around, keeping us safe from bears. In the last two years, I've seen only one small black bear across the cove from our cabin. It feels as if KittyBaby is still scaring off any large carnivores who might think of us as easy pickings!

Meditation

Do cats have any idea how little they are? Are they big souls in tiny bodies? What do they show us about the benefits of viewing ourselves without limitations?

Pete's in Heaven

Niki Behrikis Shanahan
Tyngsborough, Massachussetts

*W*hen Jack and I were first married, we lived in a second-floor condominium. Little did we know that a cat who lived on the first floor of our building would become an important part of our lives.

One day, we heard a cat meowing in the hallway. Jack dashed to the door and let him in. When I was growing up, our family didn't have pets, and I didn't give much thought to having an animal companion as an adult, so it didn't matter to me if the cat came in or not. Jack had always had cats in his family, though, so when the cat continued to visit us, meowing outside our door for admittance, Jack would always bring him inside. One day, I was writing at the kitchen table when the cat came for a visit. He got up on the chair beside me, and I found myself looking into the most beautiful green eyes I had ever seen. On other occasions, he would walk around and rub up against my legs as I washed dishes at the sink. Little by little, this short, fluffy bundle of love stole my heart.

Then it happened. I started looking forward to the cat's visits. That's when I knew I was hooked. We fed him regularly, and he would stay with us for long periods of time. One night, he didn't want to leave, and he slept on a rocking chair in the living room. Finally, I discovered that he belonged to Judy, who lived downstairs. "Your cat has been coming by to visit us," I told her, "and he stayed overnight a couple of times. I hope you weren't worried about him."

"No," she replied. "If he bothers you, just throw him out."

Judy told me that she would be getting married in a couple of months, and she didn't know what to do with this eight-year-old cat. Her fiancé had a dog who couldn't tolerate other animals. That was when I decided that we would adopt this cat who had stolen our hearts. We named him Pete, a name I had always liked. I thought "Pete Shanahan" had a nice sound to it.

At the time when we adopted Pete, Jack was going to night school and was busy most of the time, so Pete and I kept each other company. Pete would get up with us in the morning and have breakfast. He was always very vocal about being fed promptly. He slept on our bed, usually lying on my legs all night. He sat on my lap in the evening, napped in my arms, and played toy and flashlight games with Jack. Pete was a good sport. He would let us put a little rubber duck on his head, which amused us immensely. At Christmas, Pete was very cooperative when I put a Santa hat on him and asked him to pose for our Christmas card. He loved sitting under the Christmas tree. When I brought the tree into the house and leaned it against the wall before setting it up, Pete would sit under it, ready to start the celebrations right away. He loved to open Christmas presents and exchange gifts and cards with his grandma and auntie every year.

Fourteen wonderful years went by, during which time we moved from the condo to a house. One day, Pete sat in the bay window of our dining room. I went over to him and noticed a beautiful, pure-white cat outside, sitting directly in front of the window. The white cat stared up at Pete. I called Jack to come see this white cat, who seemed to be in a trance as she gazed at Pete. A couple of minutes after Jack joined us, the cat vanished from sight.

I immediately ran outside to leave some food for the white cat in case she came back. But I had an uneasy feeling that this had been no ordinary cat. There are very few outdoor cats in our neighbor-hood. We'd never seen this white cat before, and we haven't seen her since. I couldn't get the thought out of my mind that this was a beautiful feline angel, or an angel in the appearance of a cat, ready to take Pete to heaven. Later that night, I asked Jack if we could pray for Pete, and we did. Within a couple of weeks, Pete had a heart attack and passed away.

Niki's Pete

Pete had lived to be nearly twenty-two years old, which is a long life for a cat, but not enough when you love someone. He enjoyed a very loving life with us and was sick only the last year of his life. Even though it pains us deeply that he is gone, we know he's with the Lord in heaven, waiting for us to join him someday.

The great bond I shared with Pete inspired me to research the Bible to see what God had to say about the afterlife of animals. I found many relevant scriptures in my research, and I felt the need to document them in an organized way. Once I began to type them into a file, I said to Jack, "I think this is a book!" I was delighted with my findings that proved scripturally that all animals go to heaven. I titled the book *There Is Eternal Life for Animals.*[2]

On December 15, 2002, exactly one year after Pete had passed away, I was moping around the house feeling depressed. I looked out the window and noticed that it had been snowing. Later, I looked out the back window toward the place where we had buried Pete. Then I saw a cross of snow on the big rock we'd placed over Pete's grave. I wondered why there wasn't any snow on the rest of the rock; snow covered the trees, the grass, and everything else. But on the rock, the snow had only formed the shape of a cross.

After the snow melted, I went out to look at the rock and found that there was a branch on it, which had formed the vertical part of the cross. An indentation in the rock had made the horizontal segment of the cross. We have photos of the rock fully covered with snow and other photos of the rock with snow melting on it. We also now have a photo of the rock with its Cross of Snow. The branch remained on the rock throughout the winter, but we never saw the Cross of Snow again — only on the first anniversary of Pete's passing.

I know that the Cross of Snow on Pete's grave on the first anniversary of his passing was a sign from God that Pete is alive and well in heaven. He gave us this sign to comfort us and reaffirm our beliefs. I believe that God wants us to share this story with all those who are feeling pain at the loss of their animal companions. It's true that God preserves people and animals, as it says in Psalm 36:6:

Your righteousness is like the great mountains
Your judgments are a great deep
O Lord, you preserve man and beast.[3]

I often wonder what it's like in heaven and what everybody is doing. Sometimes I imagine Pete playing with the other animals there, perhaps riding a big elephant. I'm sure he's spending time with my dad, who passed away forty days before Pete did. Now, whenever I feel sad about Pete being gone, I stop and think, "I have something to look forward to. I'm going home to Pete someday, and we're going to live forever in heaven." After ten thousand years go by, I'm going to turn to Pete and say, "Well, son, what do you want to do today?"

Meditation

When a cat has passed on from this life, have there been signs (which you may have ignored or dismissed) to show you that this soul is still nearby or waiting for you?

Anna's Three Angels

Judith E. Roberson
Hockessin, Delaware

*W*hen she was only eight months old, I noticed that my beautiful dilute calico Persian kitten, Anna, had a distended stomach. She was diagnosed with feline infectious peritonitis (FIP). Upon receiving the diagnosis, I refused to give up hope. The vet told me to call when Anna stopped eating and drinking, and that he would then put her down.

I contacted a homeopathic vet, and we started treatments for Anna. In addition, Anna received chiropractic services and shiatsu massage. We also used an animal communicator to assist in conveying Anna's symptoms to the vet. More love rolled around our house than we had ever experienced before, and Anna was the reason.

As Anna became unable to manage climbing the stairs to join our family each evening in the family room, my husband suggested using the "green elevator" — our green laundry basket. We would load Anna into the elevator and, as my husband went up the steps, I would follow behind him saying, "Mezzanine, second floor!"

Each time Anna and I went to the homeopathic vet, I promised the cat that she'd be coming home with me. As we rode in the car, she would stare at me with her golden eyes and purr. Anna always seemed to enjoy sitting at traffic lights, looking out the window at the other cars.

The day came when Anna grew weaker. One evening, when my husband took her out of the green elevator, Anna went into a seizure. I called the vet's emergency number, and they gave me a location for services about an hour's ride from our home. My husband refused to have Anna die in a cage, so we decided to keep her at home that night. She rallied for another day, but then again grew weak. Soon the day came when she stopped eating and drinking. My husband and I put her to bed, and we agreed that we would take her to the vet the next day for one last visit.

The next morning, neither of us wanted to leave our bedroom and go downstairs to feed the animals for fear of what we would find. We went together and found Anna near her litter box, where she had died during the night. It was difficult for us to lose such a lovely little kitten, and we cried over her passing. She had lived with us for two whole months after her FIP diagnosis.

Judith's Anna

A few days after Anna died, I contacted the animal communicator who had been working with us during Anna's illness. The communicator said that three angels had been with Anna when she died. She also said that Nikki, one of our other Persians, had seen a white light. This all was quite shocking to me because the night before Anna died I'd had a vision during my yoga meditation. In it, I saw three angels with Anna. During the night when Anna died, I'd had another vision: I saw a beautiful, intense white light, which came to me and then disappeared. I later felt that this must have been Anna's spirit leaving. The pet communicator told me that, spiritually, I had been with Anna when she died.

My husband then told me that he'd had a dream during the night when Anna died. In his dream, he saw three Annas on a shelf. First, he saw the deceased Anna, with no shape or form. Then he saw a "stuffed animal" of Anna. And last, he saw a vase holding a beautiful red rose.

I still miss this beautiful little kitten. She taught our family so much about love and healing. She also taught us about spirituality, and she showed us that animals and humans can have a spiritual connection; we are all from one universe, and we are all connected.

Meditation

The appearance of angels, a white light, dreams — these are all ways in which animals let us know that the spirit is eternal. What mystical experiences have you had with an animal's passing? Did they confound you then? Could they comfort you now?

Mina Goes to the Light

Lee Crowe
Savannah, Georgia

*I*n October 1982, an angel cat named Mina and I found each other in an unlikely way. About to turn twenty-three, I had recently moved from Georgia and was brand-new to Southern California. I got a job almost immediately in my chosen field of animation, at a place with a young, hip, casual atmosphere.

There was already one "studio cat" there — a skinny little gray-striped cat named Gray Matter. A coworker brought in a second cat — a beautiful feminine kitty with long black hair. She was a stray from somewhere in Burbank. Everyone referred to this new kitty as "the Southern belle cat" because she was delicate and prissy and a little aloof. But she was very sweet and loved to snuggle into the neck of whoever would hold her.

Our boss was okay with having one studio cat, but Gray Matter and Southern Belle were soon wreaking havoc when they played together. Finally, Southern Belle got locked in the boss's office one night and left a little "gift" there. "No more cats!" he yelled as he burst out of his office the next morning. "These cats have to go!"

One of my coworkers took Gray Matter. It didn't take much persuasion for me to know that I should adopt Southern Belle, especially since I was a Southern belle myself. Even though I'd never had a cat because of my mother's allergies, Mom had always said, "When you grow up and are on your own, you can have a cat." That day, I knew Southern Belle would be the cat for me. I brought her

Lee's Mina

home and changed her name to Wilhelmina (Mina, for short), after the heroine in *Dracula,* to celebrate this cat's dark femininity.

Mina lived with me for the next sixteen years. She was my companion through completing an applied arts diploma at an animation school, surviving a failed marriage and several failed relationships, moving to several different homes, having numerous jobs, and living through many other highs and lows. (Along the way I got a second kitty, Yo-yo, who lived with me until her passing in 2002.) Mina was the one constant throughout my young adulthood.

In October 1998, Mina began to walk as if she were drunk. After a few checkups, she was diagnosed with a failing kidney. Since she had been my first cat, all of this was a new experience for me. Several friends told me that kidney failure had ended the lives of their aged cats, so I took Mina's diagnosis seriously.

At first, my veterinarian recommended an IV flush twice a day. I administered this myself, but I asked friends to help me hold Mina while I stuck a huge needle into the loose skin between her shoulders. Then I had to wait for the vitamin-filled liquid to drip into her system. After a while, Mina got used to the routine, and we were able to do it without help.

Her next checkup revealed that Mina's condition hadn't improved. The vet recommended a round-the-clock IV at the pet hospital. I'll never forget Mina's face when I walked in for a visit and saw her on the table with a tube stuck in her little shaved arm. She actually looked happy — not excited, but calm — as if to assure me that this was helping and I was doing the right thing. But those treatments didn't reverse the deterioration of Mina's kidney. The vet who was on duty at the time of my visit said, "She only has a couple of weeks. Just take her home, and the two of you enjoy each other."

Around mid-December, seven weeks after I brought Mina back from the vet, God blessed me with a cold so that I could stay home for several days. I was able to spend a lot of time telling Mina good-bye. At one point, I was holding her and crying.

As I held Mina, a song kept playing in my mind: the Glenn Frey song "Part of Me, Part of You," from the film *Thelma and Louise.* I couldn't quite remember the words, but I kept humming the tune. I'd start to get the CD out, but then I'd be distracted by a phone call or something else. Yet I still heard the tune. Eventually, I said to myself, "Someone wants me to hear this song." I finally played the CD.

When I listened to the lyrics, I felt that this was Mina's way of letting me know that her time was limited and she couldn't wait any longer to tell me how she felt about me. Through the song's lyrics, she told me that even though she might be going to the other side, we would always be together. In the words of this song, Mina told me that this was merely a crossroads, a time of change, but that I still had my whole life ahead of me. She was encouraging me to go on, in spite of the fact that she wouldn't be there in bodily form. It was obvious to me that this song was Mina's way of saying good-bye.

Two days later, Mina was so sick she didn't want to be held. She'd hide under the bed or in my bathroom and occasionally try to stumble around the room. That night, she was in my bathroom when I went to bed. I woke up around 3:30 A.M. to the sound of her stumbling; she'd made it to the foot of my bed. I sensed that she wanted to be with me for her passage to the other side.

I got down on the floor with Mina, and we began to communicate telepathically. I had done this with her and with other pets in the past, but never this intensely. (Usually the messages involved food, play, or potty-time for the pet, or the pet would somehow know when to comfort me.) I don't know how I knew that if I asked her questions in my mind, she would answer them. I just "knew."

Mina's voice was calm, feminine, and wise, like a benevolent queen's. I asked if it was time for her to leave. She said, "Yes." Tearfully, I reassured her and encouraged her to go ahead. I told her that it would be fine and that I would be fine. Then I dozed off lying next to her and dreamed of a tunnel with a bright light at the end. When I woke up, I kidded myself for being so clichéd. But to my surprise, Mina then communicated that she wanted me to escort her down the tunnel I had seen in my dream. I told her that I would.

I put my hand on Mina's heart and visualized the tunnel again. I saw the silhouettes of other humans and animals going toward the light. As the light filled my vision, Mina's heart stopped. Soon, she no longer breathed. Mina had left her body. When I looked into her eyes, they were like black marbles.

Mina's role as an angel in my life was to look after me in my young adulthood, to always be there for me, to teach me about two-way unconditional love, and to show me how to say good-bye to a loved one. Her passing assured me that, even when the body is no longer functioning, we continue to be loved by those who are important in our lives. Mina knew this to be true when she communicated thoughts of the Glenn Frey song to me. She wanted to be sure that I knew it, too, before she left.

Because of Mina, I realized that I needn't wait until my own body stops functioning to be with her (or any loved ones) again. Mina continues to be with me and watch out for me. She is a part of me, and I am a part of her.

Meditation

Have you had the honor of being present for the passing of a special cat from your life? Could you close your eyes now and visualize what was happening spiritually as the soul left the body? Could you ask for a dream to help you know that only the cat's physical body has left this earthly plane?

Ask Cuddles

Dear Cuddles,

Do animals go to heaven?

Sincerely,

Hopeful

Dear Hopeful,

Yes, of course animals go to heaven. And we will joyfully greet you there at the Rainbow Bridge (it does
exist!) when you arrive. That's a promise.

One more thing. (You can believe this or not, but I
happen to know from personal experience that this
does happen.) Sometimes the soul that was your sweet
kitty can't wait for a heavenly reunion with you.
This soul then rejoins you at another place and

time in a different body. If you want to know the
truth of this, look into our eyes. See if you recognize an old friend.

Our love never dies.

Forever yours,
Cuddles

The "Pet Psychic," Sonya Fitzpatrick, writes, "After animals pass over, they rest for awhile, just like humans. Then they have a decision to make: whether to stay where they are, or reincarnate and go back to the earth plane in another form to learn more."[4] Through our own spiritual experiences and insights, we've concluded that the cats who have shared our lives — Cuddles, Speedy, Feisty, and Mugsy — are old souls who returned to us for one more go-round. We are so grateful that they did!

Most cats have probably made good on their reputation and lived *at least* nine lives. Otherwise, it's hard to imagine how they could have accumulated so much wisdom in one lifetime. After all, cats' spiritual heritage is impressive. In *The Mythology of Cats,* Gerald and Loretta Hausman write, "Going back to the ancient Egyptian sun priests, we find that the archetypal cat was a sun god and moon goddess, each a deity of fecundity. Cats blessed weddings and births and were always present at death, as they carried human spirits from this world to the next. Cats were connected to the cosmos as no other animal, and because of this they granted us our own vestigial link to the spheres and the powers thereof that gave us spiritual strength."[5]

Cats are mysterious, intelligent, composed, cunning, intriguing, enlightened, obnoxious, serene, aloof, persistent, patient, and cautious — and a hundred other words that could be used to describe them. They are complex creatures who charm us with their endearing ways and mystify us with their displays of wisdom. We and our co-editors, Cuddles and Speedy, wish you a lifetime of tummy rubbing, lap sitting, tongue licking, shadow boxing, tail bristling, limb stretching, toy tussling, and high perching. May you be fortunate enough to view this world and the next from a cat's spiritual perspective!

Notes

Introduction

Epigraph: Algernon Charles Swinburne, excerpted from "To a Cat," quoted in *The Well-Versed Cat: Poems of Celebration* (Philadelphia: Running Press, 1993), p. 93.

1. Roger Caras, *A Celebration of Cats* (New York: Simon & Schuster, 1986), p. 15.
2. Carolyn Osier, "The Egyptian Mau Provides a Living Link to the Time of the Pharaohs," *Cat Fancy*, September 2002, pp. 24–26.
3. Caras, p. 120.
4. Elizabeth Marshall Thomas, *The Tribe of Tiger: Cats and Their Culture* (New York: Simon & Schuster, 1994), p. 121.

5. American Pet Products Manufacturers Association (APPMA) 2003/2004 National Pet Owners Survey, posted 11 November 2003 on www.appma.org.

6. Annette Simmons, *The Story Factor: Secrets of Influence from the Art of Storytelling* (Massachusetts: Perseus Publishing, 2001), p. 27.

Chapter One: Is Life Better When We Curl Up Together?

Epigraph: The Holy Bible, the New King James version, published by the American Bible Society (New York: Thomas Nelson, 1990), p. 652.

1. Bill Hendrick, "Psychologists Dissect Multiple Meanings of Meow," Cox News Service, Friday, 30 May 2003, posted 26 June 2003 on www.timestar.com (*Alameda Times-Star* Website); Soroya V. Juarbe-Diaz, D.V.M., "Can We Talk?" *Cat Fancy,* July 1998, pp. 41–43.

2. Jeffrey Moussaieff Masson, *The Nine Emotional Lives of Cats: A Journey into the Feline Heart* (New York: Ballantine Books, 2002), p. 40.

3. Thomas, p. 104.

Chapter Two: Do We Get Help to Heal Life's Scratches?

Epigraph: Algernon Charles Swinburne, excerpted from "To a Cat," quoted in *The Well-Versed Cat: Poems of Celebration* (Philadelphia: Running Press, 1993), p. 93.

1. Lev G. Fedyniak, M.D., "A Cat's Healing Purr," *Animal Wellness,* vol. 5, issue 6, November 2003, pp. 12–14.

Chapter Three: Were We Meant to Play with Our Littermates?

Epigraph: Lewis Carroll, *Alice's Adventures in Wonderland* (New York: William Morrow & Co. Inc., Books of Wonder, 1866), p. 93.

1. Dr. Marty Becker with Danelle Morton, *The Healing Power of Pets: Harnessing the Amazing Ability of Pets to Make and Keep People Happy and Healthy* (New York: Hyperion, 2002), p. 27.

2. W. Bradford Swift, D.V.M., "What Pets Teach Kids," *Animals*, May–June 1996, pp. 10–13.

Chapter Four: Are Cats Mirrors of the Soul?

Epigraph: African-American folk saying, quoted in *A World Treasury of Folk Wisdom*, compiled by Reynold Feldman and Cynthia Voelke (New York: HarperCollins, 1992), p. 100.

1. Mark Twain, quoted in Caras, p. 135.
2. Don Holt, Jr., *Praying with Katie: God, My Cat, and Me* (Kansas City: Andrew McMeel Publishing, 2001), p. 10.

Chapter Five: Will We Hear the Sound of a Heavenly Purr?

Epigraph: William Shakespeare, *Romeo and Juliet*, ed. by Peter Holland (New York: Penguin, 2000), p. 65.

1. Clea Simon, *The Feline Mystique: On the Mysterious Connection Between Women and Cats* (New York: St. Martin's Press, 2002), p. 63.
2. Niki Behrikis Shanahan, *There Is Eternal Life for Animals* (Massachusetts: Pete Publishing, P.O. Box 282, Tyngsborough, MA 01879, 2002).
3. The Holy Bible, p. 545.
4. Sonya Fitzpatrick with Patricia Burkhart Smith, *What the Animals Tell Me: Developing Your Innate Telepathic Skills to Understand and Communicate with Your Pets* (New York: Hyperion, 1997), p. 202.
5. Gerald and Loretta Hausman, *The Mythology of Cats: Feline Legend and Lore through the Ages* (New York: Berkley Books, 2000), p. ix.

Contributors

Chapter One: Is Life Better When We Curl Up Together?

DONNA FRANCIS, "One Lucky Cat." Donna is a deaf-education teacher, animal-assisted therapy volunteer, and therapy pet evaluator. She shares her home with two dogs and three cats, including Lucky.

RENIE BURGHARDT, "My Mother's Cat." Renie is a freelance writer with credits in books such as *Chicken Soup for the Horse Lover's Soul, Chicken Soup for the Christian Family Soul, Chocolate for Women,* and others. She lives in the country with four cats and four dogs.

MARGIE BROADRICK, "Harley, the Cat Who Changed a Facility into a Home." Margie has been the activity director at the Madison Healthcare and Rehabilitation Center for five years, where she strongly encourages families to bring in their pets to visit loved ones. Margie lives with Larry, her husband of thirty-one years, and their two dogs, Zena and Skynnard.

KATHRYN VAN MATER, "Harley, the Cat Who Changed a Facility into a Home." Kathryn, eleven years old, took the photo of Harley.

CHRISTINA LOUISE DICKER, "The Persistent Princess." Christina lives on a four-acre property with her husband and their many animal friends. She enjoys songwriting and has recorded two songs promoting animal welfare. E-mail Christina at kritters@dodo.com.au.

CAROLE S. CAHILL, "The Most Remarkable Gift." Carole is a sometime actor and therapist, a longtime writer, and a lifetime lover of animals.

TONI EAMES, "The Comfort of Cameo." Toni is an author, disability-rights advocate, and lecturer. She lives with her husband, Ed; golden retriever guide dogs, Keebler and Latrell; and cats, Kizzy, Bonzie, Cali, and Nifty.

Chapter Two: Do We Get Help to Heal Life's Scratches?

CAROL SMITH, "God's Kitty Heart Specialist." Carol works for a hospice as a social worker. She now lives with two cats, Harold and Miss Minnie. Miss Minnie hasn't walked on Carol since Carol's heart surgery.

CAROL L. SKOLNICK, "The Cat Who Made Amends." Carol is an award-winning author, columnist, educator, and group-process facilitator, and a native New Yorker. Her creative nonfiction has appeared worldwide in inspirational volumes, literary journals, e-zines, magazines, and newspapers. E-mail Carol at sput6@aol.com.

JULIE ANN MOCK, "Nurse Melanie." Julie Ann is a writer, photographer, and animal shelter volunteer who lives with one husband, one cat, one dog, two rabbits, and one horse.

JUDITH A. MORRIS, "The Presence of Willie." Judith lives in the Florida Keys with her husband, Steve, and five souls in cat bodies. All have one very special spiritual guardian.

GRACEANN MACIOLEK, "The Kinky Cat Who Chose Me." Graceann shares her life with her fiancé, David Pearson (for whom she thanks God every day), and her beloved kitty of dubious intelligence, Spike.

MS. ANASTASIA LYNN BAIMA, A.S., "A Loyal Friend until the End." Anastasia is a veterinary technologist who presently lives in Virginia with her American foxhound, Honeybear, and two cats, Snowbound (DSH) and Abigail, a Maine coon.

PATTY HALL LASWICK, "Lil Mama and Her Kittens." Patty is a retired chemistry professor living in rural western Pennsylvania. She shares her home with her beloved feline family members, Wafer, Lil Mama, Einstein, and Bohr.

Chapter Three: Were We Meant to Play with Our Littermates?

BRIAN MCRAE, "Major-League Assistance from 'the Sisters.'" Brian played ten seasons (1990–99) in major-league baseball, with stops in Kansas City, Chicago, and New York. Brian is currently a host on *Major League Baseball Radio* (MLB.com), keeping fans updated on the latest baseball information. He is the owner of radio station WHB 810 AM in Kansas City, Kansas.

KEVIN COLE, "Muse of Mirth." Kevin is a North Carolina–based writer who often enlists humor to advance the causes of animal awareness and global kindness. "Muse of Mirth" is based on an article of the author's that appeared in the fall 2002 issue of *laJoie Journal,* a Batesville, Virginia–based publication dedicated to reverence for all life.

JUDITH A. MORRIS, "Living with a Dickens." (See chapter 2, above.)

SUE STANGE, "This Candy Is Reserved for Cats." Sue lives with her three cats, including Lucy. When Sue's mom died, Sue adopted Lucy. Sue volunteers at a local animal shelter.

DARBY DAVIS, "Bam Bam Helped Me Pack for My Vacation." Darby is the publisher of *Awareness Magazine,* Southern California's largest bimonthly holistic publication, currently reaching more than 180,000 readers. For more information, see www.awarenessmag.com.

JENNY CARLSON, "A Place at the Table." Jenny lives in Minneapolis, Minnesota, with her husband, Greg, and their new baby, Shawn. They love their pets.

PAMELA V. BROWN, "Cat's Hair." Pamela is a freelance writer living in Kapaa, Kauai, Hawaii. She enjoys watching professed non-cat people be "converted" into cat people when they least expect it.

Chapter Four: Are Cats Mirrors of the Soul?

LAURIE CRAWFORD STONE, "My Patient and My Healer." Laurie is an attorney and animal advocate, published in *Voices from the Garden.* She lives with her husband, Roger, and rescued felines Keisha, Coco, Frankie, Lucy, Cooper, and Winston. Her Website is www.belovedanimals.com.

BEVERLY F. WALKER, "The Music of Forever Love." Beverly enjoys writing, quilting, and being with her grandchildren. Beverly's other animal stories appear in *Loss, Comfort, and Healing from Animal Sightings: True Experiences of Animal Blessings,* by Patricia Spork.

PAMELA JENKINS, "Tough Guy." Pamela is the office manager of her husband's veterinary clinic. She enjoys writing about the loving bond between people and their pets.

TIM BELLOWS, "A Morning Home Alone." Tim is a poet, college teacher, and writer who is devoted to wilderness and contemplative travels. A graduate of the Iowa Writers' Workshop, Tim has published work in over 140 literary journals and in *A Racing Up the Sky* (Eclectic Press). He has earned two nominations for the Annual Pushcart Prize.

BETTINE CLEMEN, "A Life Lesson from Two Cats." Bettine is an international flautist who is known for performances, books, and CDs showing the interconnectedness of life. As her music soars, visuals in her concerts depict children and animals she has met and serenaded throughout the world (see www.joyofmusic.com).

SALLY ROSENTHAL, "Hocus and a World of Ordinary Miracles." Sally is a Cat Writers' Association member; she writes for *Best Friends, laJoie,* and other publications. Sally and her guide dog, Boise, are pet therapy volunteers.

Chapter Five: Will We Hear the Sound of a Heavenly Purr?

TIM MIEJAN, "The Man Who Got His Purr Back." Tim is the editor of *The Edge,* a leading source in the United States for inspiration, education, and information related to personal growth, integrative healing, and global transformation (see www.edgenews.com).

CAROLE PUNT, "Tigger Purrs a Love Song to God." Carole is a writer for a company that manufactures health products. She and her husband are grateful for the companionship of two cats, Tigger and Mugs.

NANCY STRAND, "Bears Are No Match for KittyBaby." Nancy is the daughter of a pioneer Alaska family. She lives with several cats in her cabin at Sandy Beach, and she is studying to be an herbalist. Her e-mail address is feraltmccloud@hotmail.com.

NIKI BEHRIKIS SHANAHAN, "Pete's in Heaven." Niki is the author of *There Is Eternal Life for Animals,* which proves through Bible scriptures that all animals have an afterlife in heaven (see www.eternalanimals.com).

JUDITH E. ROBERSON, "Anna's Three Angels." Judy is a speech/language pathologist who lives with her husband and two Persian cats, Nikki (Anna's cousin) and Gabe (Anna's brother) in Hockessin, Delaware. Nikki and Gabe often happily join Judith's younger speech clients during their treatment sessions.

LEE CROWE, "Mina Goes to the Light." Mina is a former Disney artist who is currently working toward her master's degree in illustration. She shares her home in Savannah, Georgia, with her husband, Dan, and their cat, Flaubert.

Acknowledgments

*C*uddles and Speedy have been the coeditors of this book, along with our angel cats in heaven, Feisty and Mugsy. We owe them special thanks for helping us understand the cat kingdom.

We want to express appreciation to our ever-supportive and caring human families, especially Bobbie Anderson, Darrell and Gertrude Jackson, Patricia Jackson, Dominic Jones, and Mary Jackson Babel. Our children, Susan Anderson and Mun Anderson, are always in our hearts.

Special thanks to Harold and Joan Klemp for their love and constant inspiration.

We are grateful to all the authors who contributed stories and photographs of the cat friends who have enriched their lives — and ours. To Brian McRae, we are most appreciative of your patience and perseverance as you shared with us how Monster and O-fer brought joy to your life as a major-league baseball player. Thanks also to the generous people who endorsed this book.

Stephanie Kip Rostan, our super-agent at Levine-Greenberg Literary Agency, Inc., continues to offer her encouragement and wisdom with grace, perception, and great skill.

Georgia Hughes at New World Library is a writer's dream of an editor, and her suggestions always improve each project. Thanks as well to editor Kristen Cashman. We also are grateful to Carol Venolia, our most thorough and precise copyeditor. Munro Magruder steers the marketing ship with a finesse that we greatly admire. We never cease to be impressed by our charming publicist, Monique Muhlenkamp. And the beauty of this book is due in large part to the design genius of Cathey Flickinger and Tona Pearce Myers. Thanks to Marc Allen and all the staff at New World Library for giving us a home from which we can launch these stories into the world.

Many members of the media have helped bring the messages of our books to the public by writing about and interviewing us or by featuring the books on radio and television. Our special gratitude goes to Brad Woodard, Lessandra MacHamer, Sarah Casey Newman, Sally Rosenthal, Dr. Jonathan Greenfield, D.V.M., Darby Davis, Sylvia Hubbard, Alicyn Leigh, Zoh M. Hieronimus, and Willard Scott.

Dear friends have made the journey of this book so much sweeter. We especially want to thank our hero, Barbara J. Gislason, chair of the Minnesota State Bar Association's Animal Law section.

Also, we are grateful for the love and support of our dear friends: Arlene and Aubrey Forbes, Barbara Buckner, Josse Ford, Daniel Tardent, Carol Frysinger, Kristy Walker, Barbara Morningstar, Bettine Clemen, Peter Longley, Margo Hendricks, Gail Roeske, Diane Burkitt, Doug and April Munson, Diana and Henry Stewart-Koster, Catherine Gray, and Mary Carroll Moore.

Organizations and groups that have supported and inspired us include the Thursday Night Writer's Group, The ECK Writer's Group, The Loft Literary Center, and the Minnesota Screenwriters Workshop.

About Allen and Linda Anderson

$\mathcal{A}$llen and Linda Anderson are authors and inspirational speakers who have been married since 1983. They cofounded the Angel Animals Network, dedicated to increasing love and respect for all life — one story at a time (see www.angelanimals.net).

In addition to *Angel Cats: Divine Messengers of Comfort,* their books together are *Angel Animals: Exploring Our Spiritual Connection with Animals* and *God's Messengers: What Animals Teach Us about the Divine.* Their next book in this series is *Angel Dogs: Divine Messengers of Love* (New World Library, fall 2005).

Allen is a computer software trainer, photographer, and writer. He was profiled in Jackie Waldman's book *The Courage to Give.*

Linda Anderson is an award-winning playwright and screenwriter, fiction writer, and author of *35 Golden Keys to Who You Are & Why You're Here.* Allen and Linda teach writing at The Loft Literary Center in Minneapolis, where Linda was awarded The Anderson Residency for Outstanding Loft Teachers. Allen and Linda share their home in Minneapolis with a menagerie of pets, and they donate a portion of the revenue from their projects to animal shelters and organizations.

You are welcome to visit Allen and Linda's Website and to send in stories and letters about your spiritual experiences with animals for possible future publication. At the Website or by e-mail, you may also request a subscription to the free online publication *Angel Animals Story of the Week;* you'll receive a new inspiring story each week.

Contact Allen and Linda Anderson at:

Angel Animals Network
P.O. Box 26354
Minneapolis, MN 55426
Website: www.angelanimals.net
E-mail: angelanimals@angelanimals.net

New World Library is dedicated to
publishing books and audio products
that inspire and challenge us to improve
the quality of our lives and our world.

Our products are available
in bookstores everywhere.
For our catalog, please contact:

New World Library
14 Pamaron Way
Novato, California 94949

Phone: (415) 884-2100 or (800) 972-6657
Catalog requests: Ext. 50
Orders: Ext. 52
Fax: (415) 884-2199

E-mail: escort@newworldlibrary.com
Website: www.newworldlibrary.com